"Douglas Brouwer's memoir is an intelligent, candid, and absorbing account of a deeply felt ministry. He tells the truth about ministry in all its pain and joy. Absolutely compelling!"

— CORNELIUS PLANTINGA
author of *Morning and Evening Prayers*

"An absorbing account of the quibbles, foibles, hassles, and hangups of a life in ministry—which weave in and through all the joys, surprises, marvels, and vistas of a Spirit-led life. The Christian life is full of surprises, and this memoir invites us to see in each one an opportunity to 'walk in step with the Spirit.'"

— JOHN D. WITVLIET
director of the Calvin Institute of Christian Worship

"Douglas Brouwer's memoir on pastoral work is a gem and a treasure that will be known as such for a long time to come. Eugene Peterson lamented in *Working the Angles: The Shape of Pastoral Integrity*, 'Pastors are abandoning their posts, left and right, and at an alarming rate. . . . The pastors of America have metamorphosed into a company of shopkeepers.' He certainly wasn't thinking of Douglas Brouwer when he wrote that. I have known Doug for a very long time, and he is the real deal. His memoir is pure gift!"

— TIMOTHY L. BROWN
professor of preaching and president emeritus at
Western Theological Seminary

Chasing after Wind

A PASTOR'S LIFE

Douglas J. Brouwer

WILLIAM B. EERDMANS PUBLISHING COMPANY
GRAND RAPIDS, MICHIGAN

Wm. B. Eerdmans Publishing Co.
4035 Park East Court SE, Grand Rapids, Michigan 49546
www.eerdmans.com

28 27 26 25 24 23 22   1 2 3 4 5 6 7

ISBN 978-0-8028-8187-8

Library of Congress Cataloging-in-Publication Data

Names: Brouwer, Douglas J., author.
Title: Chasing after wind : a pastor's life / Douglas J. Brouwer.
Description: Grand Rapids, Michigan : William B. Eerdmans Publishing
    Company, [2022] | Summary: "A memoir of a Presbyterian pastor that
    speaks to both the joys and discouragements of Christian ministry
    in the current age of shrinking mainline churches"—Provided by
    publisher.
Identifiers: LCCN 2021038230 | ISBN 9780802881878 (paperback)
Subjects: LCSH: Brouwer, Douglas J. | Presbyterian Church—Clergy—
    Biography. | BISAC: RELIGION / Christian Ministry / General |
    RELIGION / Christianity / Presbyterian
Classification: LCC BX9225.B756 A3 2022 | DDC 285.092 [B]—dc23
LC record available at https://lccn.loc.gov/2021038230

Quotations of Scripture are from the New Revised Standard Version of
the Bible.

Contents

CONTENTS

Foreword

IN HER BOOK *BIRD BY BIRD* Anne Lamott writes: "Tell your stories. If people wanted you to write warmly about them, they should have behaved better." Douglas Brouwer places this quotation at the beginning of one of his chapters, and if another author had done that in writing about his life I might see this as a signal that the author was going to start airing some grievances. But I wasn't worried in Douglas's case. He was already more than a third of the way into his book when he introduced this comment from Anne Lamott, and there was not reason to think that he was now about to launch into some "get even" diatribes. In fact, if anything Douglas at times seems to be turning Anne Lamott's counsel back on himself. He tells the story of his life here with the awareness that if he wanted to be able to tell warm stories about himself, he should have behaved better.

Not that this is a book dominated by *mea culpa* memories. This is a marvelously candid memoir, focusing in good part on several decades of dedicated parish ministry. His telling of the story begins, though, well before that pastoral career got going. Douglas describes in some detail what it was like to be raised in the Dutch Calvinist community in Grand Rapids, Michigan, which meant memorizing the Heidelberg Catechism and attending Christian schools, followed by an undergraduate education at Calvin College.

I knew him in those Calvin days—I was faculty advisor to the Lectureship Council on which he served as student chair. In that role he reached beyond the community's normal boundaries—but with no real communal opposition—to invite as guest lecturers Anaïs Nin (a gifted writer who had once been Henry Miller's lover), Harvard's Harvey Cox, and the famed Jewish novelist Chaim Potok.

It did not surprise me, then, that when he graduated from Calvin he chose to attend Princeton Seminary rather than the Christian Reformed Church's theological school. And, having made that choice, he was on his way—not without some vocational wrestling along that way—to his service in mainline Presbyterianism. And even a little broader than that: he served two pastorates in more "ecumenical" international congregations in Switzerland.

In one sense much of Douglas's story, then, is about moving away from the "thick" ethnic-theological world of Dutch Calvinism to broader environs. But the narrative, as he tells it, is not one of rejecting his past. He took much of that past with him as he moved on. It was in his Christian Reformed Sunday school classes, he confesses to us at one point, "where I learned most of the important things about my faith."

Douglas and I have walked similar paths. I started off in that same Dutch Calvinist world but eventually joined a mainline Presbyterian church—and, like him, still belong to a congregation of that denomination. In reading his account here, I did at points sense that I have missed our shared background a little more than he does. But then the reassuring tears came for me when at the very end of the last chapter, in thanking some important people in his journey, he tells us that his kindergarten Sunday school teacher, Mrs. Peterson, "made the Bible stories come alive for me in a way no one else ever has, including some highly regarded seminary professors with whom I studied."

At a couple of points he thanks me as friend who frequently "tried to point me in the right direction." I appreciate the expression of gratitude, but I have never worried about the direction he was going. Those tears of gratitude that I just mentioned came at other points in reading this book. One instance was when he described the thrill of baptizing in Switzerland's Lake Zurich a young woman, Nadia, who raised her arms and cried out in joy, after Douglas raised her "from the icy waters of death to resurrection life." That says much about the direction of a wonderful ministry. At a number of other points in this book Douglas also points me in spiritual directions that I wish I had pursued.

But back to that piece of Anne Lamott counsel. Douglas does not ignore the difficult—even deeply disillusioning—experiences in his ministry. And it is clear that there were people along the way who failed to serve him in ways that he needed. He seldom tells these stories with any bitterness, though, and when he does get into (without naming names) an especially horrendous church staff situation, it is in reporting to us how he worked to let the bad memories go. It is refreshing to read a book of remembrances by a successful church leader who is candid about what he bluntly calls the "dumbass" mistakes he made in his ministry.

Obviously, I have personal reasons to praise this book, written by a friend whom I greatly admire. But this is a memoir that speaks to the hearts of all of us who, wherever our journeys began, can look back on the marvelous grace that has empowered "dumbass" people like us to accomplish goals for the Kingdom!

Richard J. Mouw

At the End of the Day

My quest to serve God in the church had exhausted my spiritual savings. My dedication to being good cost me a fortune in being whole. My desire to do all things well had kept me from doing the one thing within my power to do, which was to discover what it meant to be fully human.

Barbara Brown Taylor, *Leaving Church*

Tell the truth, or someone will tell it for you.

Stephanie Klein, *Straight Up and Dirty*

I was a Presbyterian pastor for forty years. I loved most of it, barely tolerated some of it, and was grateful to be finished with much of it.

Exactly two years ago I climbed twelve steps to reach an old pulpit in an old church in Zürich, Switzerland, and I preached my last sermon to my last congregation. I made the sermon more about God than about me, which I have always tried to do, and then, when I was finished, I climbed down the same twelve steps and sat in my reserved seat up front.

After the final hymn and benediction, I sat once again and listened along with the congregation to Widor's *Toccata*, the organ piece I had requested for the occasion, one of the most famous organ works ever written. And then I cried. The last part was unplanned. My tears might have been tears of gratitude, but they were most certainly tears of relief. I had just lunged across the finish line after the longest race of my life, and I couldn't quite believe that I had made it.

A few months before I retired, a dear friend, someone I have known since college days, asked me what I planned to do after I retired, and to my surprise—to hers as well—I said, "I plan to remember who I am," as though over the years I had forgotten.

These were words I hadn't planned on saying. I just blurted them out, which is how truth is often spoken. What had happened, I now realize, is that I had lost myself so deeply in a role and a title and a way of life that I was no longer sure whether I had an identity separate from those things. Church members over the years have been all too happy to tell me how a pastor should act, speak, think, pray, dress, drive, raise kids, vote, and so on. For forty years they made lots of suggestions for my behavior and appearance, even extending to what sort of car I should drive. And now I wanted more than anything to find out who I really was, if something of my old self still existed.

ONE GOOD SIGN IS that in retirement I am starting to speak once again without calibrating my words, without wondering how my words will be received, which is what I did for too many years. Not that thinking before speaking is a bad thing, but while I was thinking I would always weigh how much of what I was thinking I could say aloud. With that constraint gone, I now feel free in a way that I haven't in a long, long time. I could cry again right now just thinking about it.

I have preached a few sermons since that day in Zürich, more than I expected, but mostly my life as a pastor is over. I had a good run. My gifted young colleague, whose presence during my last years at the church in Zürich was a daily reminder that my time was just about up, leaned over during the postlude and whispered, "Forty years without a scandal. Congratulations!" I laughed. It was a good line, one I would have enjoyed saying. And mostly it was the truth, but sometimes I can't help myself: I began to wonder if it was true.

Maybe those forty years weren't a scandal in the modern sense. After all, I managed to squeak by without embarrassing myself. But maybe those years were a scandal in the older sense of the word, the New Testament sense. To cause a scandal in the ancient Greek world meant to trip someone up, to act in a way, intentionally or not, that would lead someone astray. The New Testament uses the word twenty-nine times in twenty-seven verses, so to cause a scandal, or to be a scandal, obviously isn't good. The Bible never leaves the important stuff in doubt.

Was my ministry a scandal in the older sense of the word? I've been thinking about that question—and a few others like it—pretty much nonstop since the day I sat down and cried.

IF YOU'RE A HOUSE PAINTER, then at least you have something to admire at the end of the day. If you're a pastor, on the other hand, what exactly is there to look at? I have served churches in five states— six if you count my fifteen months as an unordained "student pastor" in Iowa City. I have served a church in Zürich, Switzerland (my last), as well as a church in Harrisburg, Pennsylvania (my first). I have officiated at hundreds of funerals (a testimony, more than anything, to the average age of the membership in the churches I served). I have officiated at fewer weddings than funerals, but still more than I can count. I have attended more committee meetings than any human being should ever have to attend. I have participated in search committees to bring new staff members aboard, and I have attended personnel committee meetings where the decision was made to let staff members go. I have loved colleagues, and I have never felt more betrayed than I have been by colleagues. I have tried every day of the week, except Sunday, as a possible day off, only to land back on Monday after each attempt. I have never had a reserved parking space, but I have always had an office with a desk, some bookshelves, a couple of chairs, and (twice) a bathroom all to myself. I have been a pastor, the best one I knew how to be.

How I came to the end with a mixture of gratitude and relief continues to be a puzzle I am working on. I know the broad outline of the story, of course, but I wonder if it adds up to anything. The money I once raised to build a gym, some classrooms, and a parking lot? Was that a good idea? I thought so at the time. I poured myself into it. I made fundraising trips to Florida and California. And I neglected my family in the process. But now I wonder if those millions of dollars could have been better used on something else.

I was aware all along that I didn't choose this way of life. It chose me. If anything, I'm convinced of that now more than ever. I have always worked with a strong, occasionally overwhelming, sense of call or vocation, though there were plenty of times, early on, when I thought I was on my own and figuring things out for myself. But now that I am at the end of my useful life as a pastor, I wonder whether there has been any substance to what I did with my life, anything to admire at the end of the day.

My Grandma Brouwer's favorite book of the Bible was Ecclesi-astes. She never said so, but everyone in the family knew. That's the book she would read from whenever we gathered for dinner at her table. I wasn't sure what to make of it then, but I think I understand a little better now: "Then I considered all that my hands had done and the toil I had spent in doing it and . . . all was vanity and a chasing after wind" (2:11).

This isn't depression, and I doubt that my grandmother was de-pressed. I think this was an honest appraisal of my grandmother's life, and it might be an honest appraisal of mine.

I NO LONGER REMEMBER exactly when my sense of disillusionment with the church began. It must have happened fairly soon after ordi-nation. Every relationship almost inevitably involves some disillu-sionment. Even marriage. Maybe especially marriage. You wake up one day, take a long look at the person lying next to you in bed, and think, "Is this the person I imagined spending my life with?" There were many mornings I woke up and thought I had made a mistake by ever getting mixed up with something like the church. When a church member, for example, called the church office one Monday morning during my first year to complain about my brown shoes.

"Tell the new associate pastor to get some black shoes to wear under that black robe," she is reported to have told the church secre-tary before hanging up. The church secretary dutifully passed along the message.

Having good colleagues along the way has helped. In that first church, we invented something in my honor called the Brown Shoe Award, given as often as necessary to a member of the staff who un-intentionally irritated or offended a church member, and then at staff meetings we made a short ceremony of presenting it, accompanied by nervous laughter, knowing that any one of us could be the next recipient. Offending someone in the church is nearly impossible not to do, so I remember lots of Brown Shoe Awards that first year.

But the sense of disillusionment continued to grow. In the first church I served as senior pastor, having finally emerged from what I thought of as the lowly associate pastor role, I must have seemed discouraged one Sunday morning, because a friend, the chair of the search committee who had brought me to the church, the person who stopped by my office every Sunday morning with a prayer for me that he had typed on a 3×5 card, asked, "Have they spit on you yet?" He was referring to Jesus, of course, who was tormented by his Roman guards, and I had to admit that, no, no one had spit on me yet.

I suppose he meant to keep me going by reminding me that Jesus had it worse—that ministry, after all, is the way of the cross. And it's true, Jesus did have it worse. Being spit upon was the least of his concerns. So I coped with my disillusionment the best I could, reminding myself that suffering would be part of the call. I read books, took classes, attended seminars, and even went back to seminary for an additional degree, as though my first one was not enough. I tried my best to understand the church. I tried to be the best pastoral leader I knew how to be. And occasionally I succeeded. Just as often, though, I failed.

During my fortieth year of life, as if right on cue, I woke up one morning and decided that I needed to make a change. A *career* change. Other people made career changes, I reasoned. They regularly made appointments with me to ask the question: "What am I supposed to be doing with my life?" Why shouldn't I be allowed to do the same thing?

I said all of this to my wife, hoping that she would tell me to see a therapist instead. But to my surprise, she said, as she has said often throughout our marriage, "Okay, if that's what you want to do."

If she had pleaded with me to stay in my job because a change might upset our retirement planning or our family life, I might have given in. And then—I've seen this before in other marriages—I could have blamed her for my unhappiness, finding relief in resentment. But she was, and still is, smarter than I am. And with the responsibility cleverly shifted back to me, I made an appointment with someone who made a good living talking with disillusioned pastors.

He put me through the usual battery of tests, most of which I had taken in preparation for ordination, and then he asked me to write a short essay about what I (not others) considered to be my major accomplishments. This was a difficult essay to write, not because the words were hard to find, but because what others thought about me and my work had shaped my thinking to a far larger extent than I realized—which, in hindsight, seemed to be the point of the exercise.

The final assignment was to talk one-on-one with this professional about wanting to do something different with my life, the reason I had made the appointment in the first place. "Some days," I told him, "I feel like little more than the executive director of a nonprofit. I raise money. I encourage a staff—or try to. And I worry about lots of inconsequential things."

"Like what?" he asked.

"Like parking," I said. "When I first signed up for this work, I wanted to do ministry, to care for people, to talk about God's grace, and now what I find myself doing is listening to people complain about how hard it is to find a parking place on Sunday morning." I said more, and I could hear the whiny tone in my voice, but it's not every day that someone appears to listen carefully and thoughtfully to what you're saying. So I kept going until I ran out of steam.

Then this person said, "Hmm. Sounds like you want to get back to whatever it was you originally felt called to do."

And that was the end of it. I drove home thinking that I had made a breakthrough though, as it turned out, I had a great deal of work still to do.

I REMEMBER READING Barbara Brown Taylor's memoir *Leaving Church* and feeling irritated by it. When she was ordained, Brown reports, "Priesthood was as natural to me as breathing." That wasn't quite my experience, but I was with her at that point, enjoying her familiar descriptions of ministry and church life. I was happy about the growth she experienced at a rural church in Clarksville, Georgia. I wanted her to succeed as success had always been defined for me. But then, over time, something happened to Brown. She began to experience the demands of church life as exhausting and not at all life-giving. "Sixty-hour weeks were normal," she wrote, "hovering closer to eighty during the holidays." And so, one day, Brown walked away. Gave it all up for a life of writing and teaching.

Sixty-hour weeks were my experience too, as well as eighty during the holidays, as I imagine it is for many pastors. But the difference was that I toughed it out while she quit. For some reason I wasn't happy about her decision. I remember writing a mostly critical review of the book for a theological journal, and one day I must have complained about the book to a colleague who unexpectedly took Brown's side.

"Good for her," my colleague said.

"What do you mean?" I demanded to know.

"Well, she's not leaving God or her faith behind, is she? She simply decided to follow her call in a different, much healthier way."

I was not persuaded then, but I think I may be now. It had not occurred to me that Brown's decision was a courageous one. I wanted to see her decision as a defeat, and it's true that Brown writes about the many losses she experienced as a result of "leaving." But she also writes about what she gained: "My vocation," she writes, "was to love God and my neighbor, and that was something I could do anywhere, with anyone, with or without a collar. My priesthood was not what I did but who I was. In this new light, nothing was wasted. All that had gone before was blessing, and all yet to come was more." Brown's story, as I read it now, is a story of call not lost but reexamined and rediscovered. For much of my ministry, I was too busy seeking the way of the cross (or what I thought was the way of the cross) to understand that.

EARLIER IN MY LIFE I wanted more than anything to write a book and have it published by the time I was forty, and one day over lunch at the Schnitzelbank restaurant in Grand Rapids with the editor-in-chief of Wm. B. Eerdmans Publishing Company, I pitched my idea.

"I want to write about my work," I said. "You know, what it really looks like to be a pastor."

I knew Jon Pott well enough at the time to have lunch with him. Not many writers are lucky enough to have a conversation like this, so I was grateful for his time. He even picked up the check. But I haven't forgotten his words.

"Who are you, and why would anyone want to read your story?" he said.

The conversation soon came to an end, and Jon headed back down Jefferson Avenue to his office. I wasn't the first author whose brilliant idea for a book was shot down at an early stage. In hindsight I'm glad I waited a few years to write my story.

Who am I? I'm a pastor. Or rather, I *was* a pastor. I gave forty years to a way of life, and I gave so much of myself that I nearly disappeared inside of it.

An Utterly Normal Childhood

It may be fashionable to assert all is holy, but not many people are willing to haul ass to church four or five times a day to sing about it. It's not for the faint of heart.

Kathleen Norris,
Dakota: A Spiritual Autobiography

Each of us is a book waiting to be written, and that book, if written, results in a person explained.

Thomas M. Cirignano, *The Constant Outsider:*
Memoir of a South Boston Mechanic

I DIDN'T THINK THERE WAS ANYTHING REMARKABLE about my childhood until, as an adult, I began telling other people about it. Most children assume that their experience of childhood is widely shared, and then, later on, some of them make the disturbing discovery that it wasn't, that there was something odd or peculiar about it.

To the casual observer, my childhood might have seemed like that of most others my age. My father returned from World War II and married my mother. They bought a comfortable four-bedroom, one-bathroom ranch house in a brand-new suburb, and they set out to have three children. I was the middle child and only son. I walked to school in the morning, came home for lunch, and then went back in the afternoon, two round trips a day. My mother was always ready with my lunch, and there were never any snow days, which is remarkable for a Michigan childhood. I'm not asking for sympathy.

The school was within easy walking distance of home, but the church was even closer. In fact, I could see little else from my bedroom window. The church has continued to loom large throughout my life.

My classmates and I were third-generation immigrants from the Netherlands. Our parents and grandparents had made the difficult journey from the old country, had learned to speak a new language, and had largely assimilated into American culture. Dutch immigrants to the United States were, with only a few exceptions, hardworking and industrious, and they had succeeded socioeconomically beyond their wildest imaginations. The only vestiges of my ethnic past were special foods at Christmas and my grandfather's wooden shoes which he wore for backyard gardening. By the time I came along, we were thoroughly and proudly American.

Except for our unique expression of religious faith. We had not given up on that. One of the reasons for coming to the new world—

being desperately poor was the main reason—was to practice a rigorous, no-nonsense version of the Calvinist faith. So, oddly, we wanted to fit into American life and be different from it at the same time.

I grew up in the Christian Reformed Church in North America. There were occasional breakaway groups, like the Protestant Reformed Church and the Netherlands Reformed Church among others, groups that wanted to be even more zealous in their devotion to the Calvinist faith, but the CRC was the denomination that shaped and formed my faith. In one way or another, my faith was going to be the dominant feature of my life.

First, there was morning and evening worship, always with a large meal and nap in between. That was Sunday. We were not allowed to watch television on Sunday, and it wasn't always clear to me why not, except that the large meal and nap didn't allow much time for anything else. Plus, I learned at an early age to stretch out with a good book when I didn't feel like sleeping.

Once, when I was ten years old, my family made what seemed like an historic exception to the no-television rule. We hurried home from evening worship on February 9, 1964, and switched on our black-and-white television in time to see the Beatles, who were appearing that night on *The Ed Sullivan Show*. I wasn't sure why an exception was made for the Beatles, but it was, and I didn't complain. My family even made Sunday worship a priority when we were on vacation, so I have memories of worship in Christian Reformed churches all over the United States, many of them quite small, including one in Salt Lake City that met in the pastor's living room. I remember feeling uncomfortable there and was glad to leave.

Next, there was Sunday school every Sunday before morning worship. My kindergarten teacher, Mrs. Peterson, made a deep impression on me because she had white hair and seemed quite old, though she was probably in her early fifties. She had just returned from mission work in the far-off land of New Mexico, and so she would tell us stories about the Zuni and Navajo Indians who lived there. (The term "Native American" was not yet in use, nor had there been a reckoning with the traumatic legacy of mission schools where she had apparently worked.) Mrs. Peterson taught me to sing "Jesus loves me, this I know, for the Bible tells me so," and from then on the lyrics to that song were a fully adequate summary of my faith.

If I stopped there, my childhood might still seem similar to that of many others who found their way into the life of a pastor, but morning and evening worship, plus Sunday school, were only the beginning of my faith formation.

BEGINNING WITH THE THIRD GRADE, I began to attend weekly catechism classes taught by the pastor at my church. The idea was that my classmates and I would memorize all 129 questions and answers of the Heidelberg Catechism, the catechism being a frequently used tool in Western Christianity for passing on a summary of Christian doctrine. It never occurred to me to question why in 1961 we were memorizing a document written in 1563 because, as I mentioned, my childhood assumption was that eight-year-olds all over the world were doing the same thing. I forget when I first learned that memorizing a sixteenth-century catechism was not a universal expectation, but I know I was startled. I distinctly remember feeling sorry for those who knew so little about their faith. "Feeling sorry," of course, is another way of saying that I felt superior.

The idea behind these weekly classes was that my classmates and I would know the catechism well enough by the twelfth grade to recite it from memory in front of the elders of the church, which is what we did. And then, as high school seniors who had committed the entire catechism to memory, we were deemed mature enough, at long last, to be received into church membership and to participate in the Lord's Supper. A later-in-life observation is that memorizing a catechism is not the same as embracing it or internalizing it.

I am mostly grateful for the experience of learning the catechism, which might seem surprising, but the language of the catechism is now deeply etched into my unconscious. (I must have missed or simply accepted the anti-Catholic and homophobic sentiments found in the catechism.) In older adulthood a few words or even a sentence will come to mind as an eloquent response to something that I've seen or heard. I can still recite the first question and answer from memory:

Q. What is your only comfort in life and death?

A. That I am not my own,

but belong with body and soul,

both in life and in death,

to my faithful Savior Jesus Christ.

He has fully paid for all my sins

with his precious blood,

and has set me free

from all the power of the devil.

He also preserves me in such a way

that without the will of my heavenly Father

not a hair can fall from my head;

indeed, all things must work together

for my salvation.

Therefore, by his Holy Spirit

he also assures me

of eternal life

and makes me heartily willing and ready

from now on to live for him.

An immigrant people who came to America, and experienced unspeakable hardships in the process, needed to know about comfort in life and death. My great-grandparents, Anthony Cornelius Brouwer and Lena Stoel, lost two children to death. One was stillborn, and the other was twenty years old when she died of "cardiac asthma," the description provided on the death certificate. Though my own childhood was far more comfortable than precarious, I nevertheless knew early on that I had been given the tools to handle whatever might happen to me. How all of the hardships in my family could be construed as "the will of my heavenly Father" remained something of a mystery to me.

But catechism classes were not the end of my faith formation. I also attended Christian schools throughout my life, starting with kindergarten and extending all the way through college. I suppose you could count seminary here as well. The first graduation ceremony I ever attended that did not begin with prayer was my wife's graduation from law school. Grand Rapids had a public school system, but the Dutch immigrants who came to America wanted faith and learning to be fully integrated and therefore wanted nothing to do with the public schools. In my childhood, Christian schools were not about providing an alternative to the theory of evolution. The Dutch immigrants in western Michigan—and in several other places around the United States, including New Jersey, Iowa, and Washington State—were concerned that all of life, literature, and history (as well as science) be understood through the lens of Christian faith.

Today there are hundreds, if not thousands, of Christian schools and academies throughout the United States, but during my childhood the idea of a Christian education was still new and somewhat countercultural. At the time, Catholic schools were just about the only other alternative to public education. My parents and the parents of my classmates were prepared to pay property taxes to support the public school system in addition to the considerable tuition of the Christian schools. To them this was a sign of being set apart, chosen, elect. Not incidentally, all of my teachers, beginning with my kindergarten teacher, Miss Noordewier, were themselves products of this same system, including the same Christian college.

Each day at the Christian school consisted of an opening prayer, devotions, Bible instruction, and sometimes hymn singing, if the teacher could play the piano. There were also weekly chapel services where the entire student body and faculty gathered in the gym and sat on folding chairs to hear a local pastor speak. In second grade I memorized all the kings of Israel and Judah, the order and duration of their reigns, as well as the correct spelling of their names. I still have the gold stars to prove it. Very few of my seminary classmates—Princeton students, no less!—knew that, in the northern kingdom of Israel, Zimri overthrew Elah to become king and that Omri overthrew Zimri, who reigned for only seven days. Ahab was the son of Zimri, and he married Jezebel. Which is a story all by itself.

What strikes me now is how dedicated my parents (and others like them) were to the idea of being "in but not of" the world. We were fully assimilated within American culture, true, but in other ways we stood apart—voluntarily, proudly, and sometimes at considerable financial cost. For my parents, standing apart was evident not in where we lived or what clothes we wore or what car we drove, but in something more fundamental. We stood apart because of a belief system. Not the idea of choice, as Christian education is often depicted today, but the idea of covenant—namely, that these choices were rooted in relationships.

EVEN MY CHRISTIAN SCHOOL EDUCATION, however, is not the end of the story, as far as my Christian formation is concerned. The Dutch immigrant population in the United States wanted to stand apart in still other ways. Many of my contemporaries learned camping and other life skills from the Boy Scouts, but because that organization was not distinctively Christian—or Christian enough—the people who raised me formed their own organization known as the Calvinist Cadet Corps. We had our own merit badges and kerchiefs, our own campouts, and our own knot-tying requirements. The sister organization to the Cadets (I am not making this up) was the Calvinettes. These, and a few other organizations, existed under an umbrella known at the time as the Young Calvinist Federation. During the summers of my high school years, I even attended Young Calvinist

Conventions, including one in Bozeman, Montana, where I was able to meet teenage Dutch Calvinists from all over North America. Meeting young Calvinist girls from places like Edmonton, Alberta, was, I must say, unexpectedly exciting.

As with so many of my other childhood experiences, I considered all of this to be utterly normal, and I just assumed that other children were experiencing life in the same or similar ways. When I reached adulthood and described my experience to others, I quickly learned that none of this was normal. I began to describe my experience to seminary classmates, jokingly, as similar to growing up Amish, though the two experiences, I know, are not exactly parallel. I now forget the news story, but I remember seeing the Christian Reformed Church described one time in a *New York Times* news story as a "sect." I was startled by that word at first, but then came to see it as accurate. I grew up in a Christian sect.

As I understand it, the church-sect typology has its origins in the work of the nineteenth-century sociologist Max Weber. According to Weber, there is a continuum with protest-like groups on one end and equilibrium-maintaining groups on the other. The protest-like groups are called sects, and equilibrium-maintaining groups are establishment churches, such as the Presbyterians with whom I spent much of my life. The church of my childhood was a protest group, fiercely proud of its outlook on life and determined to claim an outsider status. "Outsider" never meant "less than," however; "outsider" nearly always meant "better than." The Dutch Calvinist world of my childhood understood itself to be better than other traditions—and in that sense it was utterly sectarian.

REMARKABLY, GIVEN THEIR INSULARITY AND PAROCHIALISM, my parents and the other people who participated in my faith formation were intellectually curious, a trait of Dutch Calvinism and the humanism of the Reformation. This seems preposterous at one level, but overall I believe that it's true. The Dutch culture of my childhood produced many fine minds, who engaged—or at least attempted to engage—the world around them. During my undergraduate years at Calvin College (now Calvin University), I was a philosophy major, not because I thought philosophy would open doors one day in the business world, but because I was aware of the extraordinary faculty in that department—Alvin Plantinga, Nicholas Wolterstorff, and Richard Mouw, among others.

I am astonished now at how long-suffering a nationally known philosopher like Plantinga was with his undergraduate students. In a class on medieval philosophy, he patiently led us through the problem of evil and introduced us to his own substantial work on the subject, which is still some of the best in the field. Later, after my graduation, Plantinga and Wolterstorff became known for something called "Reformed epistemology," which was an argument that belief in God can be rational and justified, even without arguments or evidence for the existence of God. Plantinga's lectures were always so clear that he made me believe I knew exactly what he was talking about, and some of the time I did.

Plantinga later moved on to teach at the University of Notre Dame, while Wolterstorff left to join the faculty at Yale University. Mouw would one day become president at Fuller Theological Seminary. For a brief time, though, they and a few others were at the heart of the philosophy faculty at Calvin, and they were my teachers.

I ARGUED IN A SERMON NOT LONG AGO that my parents should get an award for providing me with the most thorough Christian formation it is possible to give a child, and no one disputed the point. (Some of those who heard me had grown up with the same experiences I had.) The thing is, my parents were only doing what all the other parents in the world of my childhood were doing. They were fulfilling promises they had made at baptism. Raising children in this way wasn't heroic; it was the expectation.

One, perhaps inevitable, result of this early experience with Christian faith is that I moved into adulthood experiencing my faith as an unlikely blend of warm piety and intellectualism. I was deeply suspicious of any other way. I knew the Bible, I knew Christian doctrine, and I knew how to make arguments in defense of my beliefs—or else knew how to thoroughly critique what others claimed to believe. But I did not always make a solid connection with Christian experience, with how I was supposed to live out the Christian faith (an issue to which I will return in a later chapter). As it turns out, my faith formation was not complete the night I recited the catechism for the elders at my church.

All this attention to knowing, understanding, and being able to think about something like Christian faith definitely shaped the kind of person (and preacher) I would one day become, a preparation that, it seems to me, has mostly served me well. Occasionally, though, my experience of faith was so different from the people I served that I had to work hard to connect.

In the last church I served, in Zürich, Switzerland, a Dutch couple made an appointment to see me one day in my office. They were not Dutch-American; they were from the Netherlands and were, like most Dutch, excellent English speakers. They were relatively new to the faith, having embraced Christianity as adults, after university, and to their credit they were very, very serious about it. They wanted to absorb everything about faith as quickly as they possibly could. Which might seem like a preacher's dream come true, but my preaching, they said, was not connecting. They were looking for certainty, for simple, declarative sentences, so that they would leave each Sunday with their faith strengthened, and I insisted (they said) on asking questions. I preferred to examine biblical truths from all angles. I seemed determined to consider all possible explanations before finally giving the conclusion, which is all they really wanted.

When they were finished with what they thought was a devastating complaint about my preaching, they looked at me expectantly, hoping that I would agree with them and that I would promise to do better. What I wanted to say was, "Thank you! My teachers would be so proud of me to hear you say that."

I realized in that moment, though, that what I loved to do, what I had been raised and trained to do, was to take an important question, a question of eternal significance (as I had learned to think of it), and then wrestle with it until it yielded truth, until the truth became obvious. I have always enjoyed hearing sermons like that, and for much of my life I would like to think that I preached sermons like that. Where I grew up, this was what we always looked forward to and expected. My faith had been formed in the tradition of Augustine and Anselm, faith seeking understanding, faith seeking a deeper *knowledge* of God. I might have said with Anselm, "I do not seek to understand in order that I may believe, but rather I believe in order that I may understand."

Imagine my astonishment to discover that not everyone in the church wants a faith characterized by the same intellectual curiosity.

My Career in Christian Publishing

We all come from the past, and children ought to know what it was that went into their making, to know that life is a braided cord of humanity stretching up from time long gone, and that it cannot be defined by the span of a single journey from diaper to shroud.

Russell Baker, *Growing Up*

History is written by the victors, but it's victims who write the memoirs.

Carol Tavris,
Mistakes Were Made (but Not by Me)

MY FIRST JOB WAS ONE FAMILIAR to many other boys in my hometown of Grand Rapids, Michigan. Every day I delivered the *Grand Rapids Press* to about a hundred houses in my neighborhood—in rain, snow, sleet, even the occasional sunny day. Rolling up and tossing the papers onto front porches was the easy part of the job. More demanding, and far more interesting, was going to each house in the evening every two weeks and collecting money. I learned a great deal about how my neighbors lived, and what they cooked for dinner, by standing just inside their front doors and waiting to be paid.

Delivering papers on Sunday morning presented a moral issue for my parents, which I solved by finding someone to deliver the papers for me. Why getting someone else to work on the Sabbath was morally acceptable to my parents, I don't remember. But the strategy worked, until my friend, the one who didn't mind working on the Sabbath, turned out to be unreliable. Eventually, to end the phone calls before church on Sunday morning from neighbors who did not receive their papers, I was allowed to deliver on Sunday mornings as well, which was a far better, albeit morally compromised, arrangement.

My next job, my first summer job, was to clear out tomato vines, hundreds and hundreds of them, from a greenhouse not far from where I lived. The work was hot and dirty, and it only lasted for a couple of weeks in August, but I was paid in cash at the end of each week. My parents never told me that I should have a job, and I don't remember that I was ever in need of money. But the thought of having a job and money in my pocket must have seemed appealing. I wasn't saving money to buy anything in particular, except my freedom. I think having a job and making a few dollars felt, at the time, like my ticket to a bigger adventure.

After the greenhouse, I worked two summers for Broekstra's Lawn Care. No one used the "mow, blow, and go" language then, but that's mostly what we did. We could easily finish ten to fifteen suburban lawns in a day. The owner, Mr. Broekstra, paid us in cash at the end of the week (there was never any tax withholding or social security deductions), and no one, as far as I knew, complained about receiving an envelope full of bills. Mr. Broekstra pretended to be irritated when a few of the boys (I was one of them) quit in mid-August to play high school football, but I think he was actually glad to see us leave when the grass was growing more slowly and the workload was lighter.

Between lawns on hot days, the crew often went for a swim in Reeds Lake, or we jumped off the Thornapple River Drive Bridge, a historic camelback bridge, for a cooling soak in the Thornapple River. I wore cutoff jean shorts and work boots every day, and I have never been as tan (or as skinny) as I was then. My medical history now requires that I make annual visits to the dermatologist, and the reason can probably be traced to this summer job when so much of my skin was exposed so much of the time. I remember coming home at the end of the day, taking a shower, and having no energy for anything. I was glad to be in bed by nine o'clock every night. My parents rarely had to worry about me being in before my curfew. In fact, I don't remember that I ever needed one. In this way, I was one of the good kids.

After my career in lawn care, I found work with the Vander Kodde Construction Company. As with previous summer jobs, I didn't really have to apply for this one. Mr. Vander Kodde had been my Little League coach for a few seasons and knew whatever he needed to know about my work ethic.

Something about "working in construction" sounded manly to me, and people always seemed impressed when I told them what I did. The reality for summer workers, though, is that the work consisted mostly of shoveling dirt and pushing wheelbarrows. Vander Kodde Construction had an in-ground pool business, in addition to its other businesses, and I was assigned much of the time to installing pools. Getting the pool into a backyard generally took about a week, and at the end of the week no homeowners ever invited the filthy crew to take a swim. We usually drove off as the pool was filling with water from a nearby fire hydrant.

Vander Kodde also built steel buildings, and when I was assigned to this work, I learned a few things about carpentry that have stayed with me. I learned how to pound a nail, for example, though most carpenters today rely on nail guns powered by air compressors. I could drive a spike into a piece of wood in two, usually three, whacks. The older guys never needed more than two whacks, and they always drove their nails straight into the wood. If they did bend a nail, which was rare, they would nearly always say, "Four eyes bend the nail," meaning that if I hadn't been watching, the nail would have gone in straight.

High school and college students typically joined the work crews in late spring or early summer, and the guys who worked year around would let us know how little we knew about construction or, for that matter, about life. So, at lunch time we would listen while they tried their best to school us about the ways of the world. One old carpenter used to sing in the morning, not out of joy, but to get a laugh from the summer help. "I wonder who's kissing her now" was one of his early-morning favorites. I don't remember the rest of the words, and it's possible that there weren't any, but we were supposed to imagine that his wife was at that very moment home in the arms of her lover. The song never seemed all that funny to me, but I was too scared not to laugh. I learned to be respectful to those for whom this was full-time work.

Another life lesson I learned was that I should never walk anywhere on the construction site without carrying something. Even if I was headed to the portable toilet, I should have something in my hand, otherwise it would look as though I was goofing off. So goofing off wasn't the problem; it was the *appearance* of goofing off that I should avoid. Whenever I walked anywhere, including to the portable toilet, I made sure that I looked purposeful by having something in my hand. Related to this life lesson, curiously enough, was the disdain that the guys in our crew held for unions. "One guy works, while three guys stand around and watch," they would say. Over time this would become a mantra, and I sort of believed it, though I had never seen an example of it. Union workers apparently didn't try to look purposeful when they were standing around or going to the portable toilet.

Summer workers typically worked too fast, and the rest of the crew would use a stretching gesture, which looked like pulling a piece of taffy from both ends. The gesture meant that we should make the work last. Getting the work done too quickly was bad and might result in being laid off. So I learned to work hard, but not too quickly. I learned to appear to be doing something at all times, even when going to the portable toilet. And I learned to mock the union guys who hardly worked at all.

Vander Kodde never discussed his political beliefs when he was my Little League coach, but at work things were different. It turned out that Vander Kodde believed strongly in George Wallace—the presidential candidate and four-term governor of Alabama. When Wallace ran for president in 1972, his second campaign for president, he made a stop at the Kent County International Airport (now the Gerald R. Ford International Airport), and Vander Kodde generously made it possible for his entire company, including the high school and college students, to go to the airport, cheer for the governor, and be paid for doing so. We were even invited to make the trip in company-owned vehicles.

I don't remember what Wallace said in his brief visit to the airport in Grand Rapids, because for some reason I didn't go. I do recall that Vander Kodde was very proud to have two dozen or so of his own people in the small crowd that assembled that day. My political beliefs were still taking shape at the time, so I might have gone just to see Wallace, if I hadn't had something else to do. To my parents' credit, they raised their eyebrows when I told them how my work buddies spent the afternoon. I know my parents sympathized with a few of Wallace's political beliefs, but they would never have gone to one of his campaign stops. Their votes that year most likely went to Richard Nixon, who was able to position himself as a moderate because of Wallace's campaign.

MY SEARCH FOR SUMMER JOBS always began sometime in the spring, and toward the end of my sophomore year of college I was having a hard time finding a job. I didn't want to work anymore in construction, and remarkably I don't think I had ever considered a restaurant job. Many people I know consider their restaurant work to have been an important rite of passage, but that was one low-wage job I never considered, possibly because it might involve nighttime hours.

Instead, I must have felt desperate enough about finding a job to ask my father if there was anything available at his company. My father never suggested that his children would be welcome in his world and never made an attempt to bring us into the advertising business. The Jaqua Advertising Agency was always a distant reality that the family would often hear about at the dinner table. My father would sometimes mention the people at work who had interesting-sounding names. "Mr. Merchant"—or often just "Merchant"—was the president of Jaqua through much of my childhood, before my father succeeded him. "Irby" and "Gus" seemed to be two of my father's close work friends, but I don't think my sisters and I ever met them. "Marilyn" worked at Jaqua and even came to our house one evening to babysit us, but I never knew what "Marilyn" did at Jaqua.

As a young child, I went to Jaqua one Saturday morning so that my father could finish a project he was working on. He set me up at a drawing table with paper and markers, and I remember feeling very important to be working alongside my father that morning in the art department. But that one time was as close as I ever came to working at Jaqua.

My father always came home from work with an interesting odor. Part cigarettes, part chemical. The chemical smell, I learned later, was from a spray fixative he used in his drawing. At home he would change into more comfortable clothes, and the odor would be gone, but that distinctive odor would appear again the next day. My father smoked during his service with the Seabees in World War II, but he seemed to have quit when the war was over. I think he smoked occasionally after the war whenever he played cards with his high school friends, but he was never a regular smoker that I recall. It's possible that he occasionally smoked at work too, or else others around him were smokers.

To a young child, the stories and odors from my father's workplace seemed interesting because they were so far removed from the worlds of home, school, and church, which were the only worlds I knew. My own workplace, the church, was never much of a mystery to my daughters. They spent lots of time there—too much, according to them—and they often knew the building (especially its hiding places) better than I did. I don't think there were any odors associated with my work.

Reluctantly, I think, though maybe with my mother's encouragement, my father agreed that spring to find a summer job for me at Jaqua, possibly in the catalog department. I made one visit to the catalog department, where I met the person in charge and where the work was explained to me, and I remember expressing great appreciation for the opportunity. I have no memory anymore of what exactly the work in the catalog department involved. But I think I could sense that this job, whatever it was, would not be a good fit for me.

Within a week I had found another job, this one at the Wm. B. Eerdmans Publishing Company, on Jefferson Avenue, near downtown Grand Rapids.

I forget now how I heard about this job, but everything about it seemed perfect. I interviewed with Glen Peterson, the sales promotion manager, and he offered me the job. I don't think there were other candidates. For the first time in my life I would be working in an office. I would shower *before* going to work, and I would not have to shovel dirt, push a wheelbarrow, or sweat. And I would not be going to the airport to meet presidential candidates. Instead, I would be writing, something I had always wanted to do. It's hard to express how perfect I thought this job was for me. I had been hired because I knew how to string a few words together in a way that made sense to other people, something I knew that I could do. And I was going to be paid for it.

My job, as it turned out, involved mornings in the sales promotion department and afternoons in the editorial department, essentially two part-time jobs mashed together.

In sales promotion I wrote catalog copy—in other words, brief descriptions of books I had never read. The spring and fall catalogs were enormously important, and so I would write about forthcoming books based on one-page, single-spaced summaries provided by the editorial department. There were other catalogs and sales items that I wrote for as well. I was even allowed to write jacket copy for one of our fall releases, though it was heavily edited, and the final version didn't look anything like what I had originally written.

And then, every Friday, someone from the printing department walked around with a stack of books, dropping one off at each desk. These were the new releases, just off the press, each one the culmination of months, sometimes years, of work. I found everything about life at a book publishing company to be thrilling, including morning coffee in the employee break room.

In the editorial department I was assigned a mostly empty office with boxes of manuscripts on the bookshelves behind my desk. The manuscripts, I learned, were articles for the *International Standard Bible Encyclopedia*, which detailed every important word in the Bible. My job, for the summer, was to read each article in the *ISBE* and watch for citations. In other words, in the article on "Adam" there might be the citation "see Eve," and I had to search the manuscript boxes to make sure there was in fact an article on "Eve." For the first week or so, this work was as thrilling as my morning work, but then after the first week less so. By the end of the summer, I was no longer quite as thrilled about being in a windowless office by myself, reading more than two hundred articles in a Bible encyclopedia. Besides, with a computer, which were not in use then, the job could probably have been done in one afternoon. The upside, of course, was that I knew quite a bit more about the Bible by the end of the summer than I had known before.

Beyond that, I could go out for lunch every day with other employees, I met and got to know the editorial staff, I mingled with everyone each morning in the break room, and I was even invited to play on the company softball team.

We called ourselves the Amazing Grace, and we played in the city recreational league. I don't remember whether we were any good or even if we won any games. What I do remember was hanging out with people I admired, people who made important decisions in the world of Christian publishing. Marlin Van Elderen was Eerdmans' editor-in-chief at the time, and I got to play slo-pitch softball with him. I was also invited to join everyone, after each game, at the Last Chance Tavern and Grill on Burton Street. I had driven by hundreds of times with my parents and always thought the place looked kind of seedy. But that summer I became a regular customer, drinking pitchers of beer with Marlin and my other buddies from Eerdmans.

The drinking age briefly dropped to eighteen in the early 1970s, along with the voting age. The thinking was that if young men were old enough to die for their country in the jungles of Vietnam, then they were old enough to drink beer and to vote. This logic made sense until there was a sudden rise in drunk driving accidents among younger drivers, and then the drinking age reverted to twenty-one—happily, a few years after I turned twenty-one.

IN MY EXCITEMENT OVER BEING INCLUDED so fully and comfortably in the world of Christian publishing, I must have overlooked how much of it I didn't like. I liked spending time in the break room, as I mentioned, and I liked playing on the company softball team. What these activities had in common was being with other people—and, notably, people who liked writing. What I didn't like nearly as much was being by myself in a windowless office, reading manuscripts, which turns out to be one of the more important parts of book publishing.

I wasn't able to see this at the time, and it was not until my first church experience that I recognized what a bad fit publishing would have been for me. And yet, publishing was what got me to seminary.

My boss in the editorial department was Edgar W. Smith Jr., the project editor for the *ISBE*. I remember seeing on the wall of his small office a diploma, a PhD, from the Claremont School of Theology. He and I didn't talk much about it, but I assumed that a degree from a good theological school must be the key to employment in the world of Christian publishing. My thinking about all of this wasn't clear at this point, but my summer work at Eerdmans was the reason—or, rather, justification—for going to seminary. I wasn't about to admit at this point in my life that my interest in seminary had anything to do with a career as a church pastor.

4

Chaim Potok's Smile

The liberty I loved was merely that of a runaway.

Saint Augustine, *Confessions*

Sometimes I have loved the peacefulness of an ordinary Sunday. It is like standing in a newly planted garden after a warm rain. You can feel the silent and invisible life.

Marilynne Robinson, *Gilead*

I'm almost certain that I went to seminary to avoid hearing the voice of God. I went to seminary to avoid hearing much of anything except what I wanted to hear. Going away to school—or just going away—was for me, I thought, the necessary first step for figuring out what to do with my life. And yet, I must have known that God had already spoken to me just as clearly as God had spoken to Moses and Mary and all the other people whom God has decided to call over the years. A better example to cite here, of course, would be Jonah. Like him I was headed to Tarshish, which advertises itself as being in the opposite direction of God's call. I figured it would be interesting to go and look around.

Already then, I must have known that I had been called and that I was running away from my call. Getting me to admit that, though, took another couple of years. In the meantime, I told myself that I was probably heading to a career in Christian book publishing or an editorial position with a Christian magazine. I look back and realize now that I was lying to myself. I was never going to do anything with my life other than be a pastor.

I'm aware that some people never leave home. They never venture very far from where they grew up. And they seem to turn out just fine. This is true for most members of my family. They appear to live normal, healthy, and productive lives. I confess that I don't understand it, and I am suspicious of it, but there it is. I, on the other hand, have always needed to be on the move—in order to grow up, find out who I was, and see a little of the world. Somehow, I always knew that I would be leaving, one way or another.

When I graduated from high school, my parents asked me what I wanted for a graduation present. They were guessing that I would ask for an electric typewriter to type college term papers; to their surprise, I told them I wanted to go to Europe. Which is where we went for a three-week tour of European capitals—my parents, my younger sister, and me. I had imagined going by myself, but my parents were not about to let their seventeen-year-old son travel by himself and traipse around another continent. So I acquired my first passport and had my first glimpse into cultures other than my own. I toured museums, cathedrals, and battlefields. I was so glad to at last leave my hometown behind, even if it was only for three weeks.

I preached an Easter sermon one time in which I mentioned the number of times a form of the verb "to go" is used in Matthew's version of the resurrection story. (Sounds fascinating, doesn't it?) After encountering the disciples outside the tomb, for example, Jesus said to them, "Do not be afraid; go and tell my brothers to go to Galilee; there they will see me." I asked my congregation that morning where Galilee was in their lives, thinking that this would be a helpful and probing question. "Where is God directing you to go?" I asked in front of large crowds at 8:00, 9:30, and 11:00. Most people on Easter morning just want to be part of a big celebration, smell the lilies, hear good music, and then go to brunch. But I insisted on making my point.

The truth is that I have always wondered where Galilee is in *my* life. I can see now that much of the time I preached for my own benefit. Sometimes, as William Willimon puts it in his memoir, *Accidental Preacher,* the one giving the sermon is the one who most needs converting. If I had followed the logic of the biblical story, I would have noticed that the disciples didn't really go anywhere, at least not at first. Instead, they went home, back to their nets, back to what was familiar. Turns out, that's where God meets us much of the time. But how was I to know that unless I left home?

DURING MY SENIOR YEAR AT CALVIN COLLEGE (now Calvin University), I chaired what was known as the Lecture Council, which brought well-known—and just as often not-so-well-known—speakers to campus each month. Along with student-produced drama and a remarkable (for its time) film series, the lecture series was meant to cultivate an intellectual life in the student body, introducing ideas and ways of thinking that most students had never considered—one purpose, as I understand it, of a liberal arts education.

I'm no longer sure why I sought or accepted this position or what I expected to make of it, but I do remember thinking at the time, as I do now, that my real education, the best learning I would do as a college student, would not be in the classroom, taking the required classes in biology and symbolic logic, but rather in extracurricular activities, like the college newspaper and literary journal, where I also spent considerable time during my undergraduate years.

The Lecture Council would meet in the late spring, just before the end of the semester, to choose themes and speakers for the following year, and then as chair I was left to make all the arrangements, which included driving to the airport in my 1968 AMC Javelin to fetch the speakers, host them during their overnight stay, and then deliver them back to the airport the next day along with their speaking fee and a thank-you note in a sealed envelope.

As chair I also stood on stage in the Fine Arts Center, introduced the speakers, and gained some early and invaluable experience in public speaking. During the fall series, I remember introducing Harvey Cox, a somewhat controversial figure at the time from Harvard Divinity School. In my introduction, I mentioned that Cox was born in 1929 in Malvern, Pennsylvania, but then noted in a deadpan that "very little is known about his early life," before moving on to mention his various books and academic achievements. That line got a laugh, as I had hoped it would, and I still find it satisfying all these years later. The line also seemed to catch Cox's attention because, after he stepped to the podium, he noted that very little was known about *my* early life either. It's hard to say why I found this moment so satisfying, except that at the age of twenty I was finding my voice and starting to enjoy it. Words, both written and spoken, had a kind of power that I was just beginning to explore.

Among other speakers during the spring semester, in a series on contemporary writers, I met and hosted Anais Nin and Lawrence Ferlinghetti. Looking back, I am surprised that no one on our Christian college campus, as far as I knew, objected to Nin, who supported herself early in her career by writing what was called "erotica" and who once carried on what was called a "bohemian relationship" with the author Henry Miller. It's hard to imagine that many Christian colleges today would be enthusiastic about this invitation. Our faculty advisor, Richard Mouw, who would leave Calvin in a few years to become president of Fuller Theological Seminary, said nothing at all about our choice and issued no warnings about possible pushback from conservative alumni. Things were different in those days in ways I did not fully appreciate.

My only memory of Ferlinghetti, a beat poet and cofounder of the City Lights bookstore in San Francisco, was of taking him, along with other members of the Lecture Council plus our faculty advisor, to a one-star Mexican restaurant on South Division Avenue, in what was not at the time an especially desirable part of town. We chose the restaurant, which no longer exists, because we thought it was the most like San Francisco our small city had to offer, though most of us had never even been to San Francisco. But if Ferlinghetti appreciated our modest attempt at hospitality, it was not obvious to me. I realize now that he was most likely looking forward to his honorarium and getting back home.

The speaker who made the longest-lasting impression on me was Chaim Potok, whose early novels explored the relationship between Orthodox and Hasidic Jews in New York City, a rather narrow slice of American life. It didn't strike me as particularly strange then, certainly not as strange as it does now, that books like *The Chosen*, *The Promise*, and *My Name is Asher Lev* would be such favorites among the Dutch Calvinists I knew in western Michigan. Many of us who read his novels found that his descriptions of the insular and intellectually stifling world of conservative Judaism in New York City were also helpful descriptions of the Dutch Calvinist world many of us experienced in western Michigan. When the main character of his novels tried to break free from the only world he had ever known, we identified with the struggle. I know I did.

There is a touching scene at the end of *The Chosen* where Danny Saunders, having grown up in a Hasidic Jewish family, has shaved his beard and cut off his earlocks, deeply disappointing his rabbi father. Danny's friend Reuven Malter watches him walk away and observes his friend as "tall, lean, bent forward with eagerness and hungry for the future." He wasn't going far geographically, but he was traveling light years from where he had grown up. And I, of course, very much wanted to be Danny Saunders, "bent forward with eagerness and hungry for the future." I was already tall and lean.

When we tried to explain all of this to Potok, I remember a strong and mostly negative response. He seemed irritated. Our little pocket of ethnic culture, even with its occasional pretentions to intellectual rigor, he seemed to say, had nothing at all in common with the world he was writing about. We didn't press the issue, because we were typically nicer and more gracious to outsiders than we were to our own, but we clearly left him wondering about us. His response left me wondering about us, too. I didn't wonder if the world he wrote about held any insights for me; I already knew that it did. Instead, I wondered what it would mean to break free of the culture in which I had been raised.

On the way to the airport after his short stay in western Michigan, in my Javelin, Potok asked me about my plans after graduation. I told him that I had been accepted for graduate study at Princeton Theological Seminary and planned to attend the following September. This choice, I mentioned, had not been encouraged by the faculty advisor to the Lecture Council. He thought about this as we drove, and when I glanced over at him I could see a smile. I don't remember that he said anything, but his smile has stayed with me all these years. It meant more to me than my newly autographed copy of *The Chosen* which

I still have on the shelf above my desk. I like to think that he did understand, after all, what his novel had meant to me.

MY FIRST TWO YEARS AT PRINCETON were challenging. I had left behind a world I knew well and had traded it for a world where no one knew me or seemed to care all that much about me. Most people had never heard of the college I had just graduated from or the denomination I was then a part of. I was one of several hundred master of divinity (MDiv) students who, like me, were finding their way in the world. Most had previous experience with living away from home, a few were married, some were financially supported by their home churches, and all of them seemed to be much more certain of their future than I was.

I enjoyed my classes in the sense that I was thoroughly engaged by them—not that I didn't struggle at times with what I heard. Some of what I learned in Sunday school needed to be dismantled and rebuilt on a stronger foundation, which can be a harrowing time for some students. Occasionally that was also true for me. My undergraduate introduction to the Old Testament class introduced me to the historical-critical method, and so I already knew, for example, that most ancient Near Eastern cultures had creation myths and flood stories. I was even prepared for the notion that the first five books of the Old Testament were not written by Moses but were mostly likely the product of several oral traditions stitched together either during or shortly after the exilic period.

To some of my classmates, however, all of this was unwelcome and even threatening information. Many of them had come to faith in campus ministries and had therefore arrived on campus with little biblical training. A few spoke up in class and argued with our professors. Going up against a tenured faculty member at Princeton in class always seemed to me to be a foolhardy thing to do, and the arguments were never very convincing, though these classmates must have felt some satisfaction they had dared to speak while the rest of us, like sheep, were silent.

My father called me once on a Sunday afternoon and asked if I had ever heard "the theory" that there were two creation stories in Genesis, that the creation story seems to start all over again in 2:4. His pastor had apparently mentioned this fact in a sermon that morning, and the information had troubled my father. He didn't doubt that it was true (he liked and trusted his pastor at the time); his question to me was, "Why weren't we ever told about this?" I sometimes wonder the same thing. Most churchgoers, I have found, are grateful to be treated like adults. I wish I had trusted this instinct in my preaching and teaching more than I did. Some references to historical-critical information might have been helpful to my church members, even if they might also be disconcerting, as I discovered with my father.

MOST OF MY CLASSMATES WORKED in churches on Sunday mornings, while I stayed behind on campus and read the Sunday *New York Times*. I couldn't see myself leading church youth groups, which is what most of these part-time job descriptions involved, so I chose instead to stay behind, read the paper, and drink coffee. A life of luxury, I must say.

What I didn't seem to grasp, for the better part of two years, was that I couldn't graduate without at least some experience of working in a church. My Wednesday afternoons and evenings as a student chaplain at Holmesburg Prison in Philadelphia were a helpful and even formative experience for me personally, but they did not meet the requirements for graduation. To graduate from seminary, students were required to have experience in the church. How did I miss that?

I had nothing in particular against the church. I wasn't planning to leave it behind. I just didn't see myself working within it. I was headed into religious publishing or editorial work. Leading the church youth group was something I never wanted to do, though years later I came to realize how much I enjoyed going on mission trips with the youth. I now realize that my avoidance of church work during those two years at seminary was a kind of magical thinking. Everyone else seemed to know what I was doing at seminary, but I imagined that I was doing something quite different. Until the little matter of graduation forced the issue.

And so, between my second and third years of seminary, I found a job in a church in the denomination in which I had been raised. I don't remember an interview, but there must have been one. The position was funded by the "home missions" board of the denomination, what would now be labeled "new church development" or "church planting." I was hired to be the student pastor at Trinity Christian Reformed Church in Iowa City, Iowa. This location, I thought, had the advantage of being far from the seminary (in a place where no one I knew would hear me preach my first sermon) and in a university town, which sounded appealing. Also, I would be working with an experienced pastor named Al Helder, who was also a licensed therapist and worked part-time for extra income in a local psychology practice. The congregation was described to me as a mix of university faculty, graduate students, and people who lived and worked nearby. There was even a farmer—Bob Faber, who invariably slept during morning worship because he had been up early to milk the cows. Perfect, I thought.

I should probably mention that I had been married about a month before this position began, maybe another reason that my magical thinking was about to end. Marriage, among all its fine qualities, offers a strong dose of reality. My life on the third floor of Alexander Hall in Princeton, New Jersey, where I enjoyed those leisurely Sunday mornings, had come to a sudden and dramatic end. I was now a husband, which carried with it the expectation that I would have an actual plan for the future.

The Iowa City church changed my life, or rather God changed my life through the Iowa City church. I left that church a changed person, with a vastly different vocational direction. I came to fulfill a graduation requirement, and I left knowing what I was going to do with my life. Student internships are designed to deepen a student's understanding of ministry, by working alongside and observing a seasoned pastor. For me the internship showed me, clearly and unmistakably, what I should be doing with my life. But I'm getting ahead of myself.

I Was No Elijah Parish Lovejoy

It follows that if you believe at fifty what you believed at fifteen, then you have not lived—or have denied the reality of your life.

Christian Wyman, *My Bright Abyss*

Develop enough courage so that you can stand up for yourself and then stand up for somebody else.

Maya Angelou

I MADE THE DECISION TO ENROLL AT Princeton Theological Seminary on the basis of a letter of admission from Arlo D. Duba, director of admissions. He had a distinctive, one-of-a-kind signature, and I studied that signature carefully, the way prospective students today might visit the campus and tour the fitness center.

The first time I saw the seminary was the day I drove up in September 1975 with all my worldly belongings, which included a potted plant my girlfriend had sent along with me. A room on the third floor of Alexander Hall was to be my home for the next two years. Today, Alexander Hall is a residence hall with seventy-nine rooms for both male and female students, but for a long time it housed the entire seminary, with meeting rooms, offices, and chapel. And, of course, there were no female students.

Princeton turned out to be a nice place to live, and by "nice" of course I mean that it is one of the most affluent communities in the United States. Princeton today is also home to several schools, including the well-known Ivy League university, with alumni such as F. Scott Fitzgerald, Michelle Obama, Brooke Shields, and Jeff Bezos. The university was founded in 1746 and was originally known as the College of New Jersey. The seminary, which was founded in 1812, is directly adjacent to the university, but from the beginning the two have been entirely separate institutions.

Princeton is also home to the Institute for Advanced Study, made famous by, among others, Albert Einstein, who once lived just a short walk down Mercer Street from Alexander Hall.

My decision to go Princeton, and not Fuller Theological Seminary where I had also been accepted, came down to money. Princeton offered to pay the lion's share of my tuition and housing cost, while Fuller did not. So, in that sense, the decision was easy. Princeton's endowment today is worth more than a billion dollars, making it the best endowed seminary in the United States. I don't know what the endowment was in the 1970s, but even then it was obvious that the seminary had a great deal of wealth. I had also applied to Harvard Divinity School, but my application file remained incomplete because Richard Mouw, my faculty advisor at Calvin, decided not to complete the letter of reference. His explanation was that "I would recommend you to them, but not them to you."

I wasn't sure at the beginning if I would fit in at Princeton. I wasn't Presbyterian, after all, and most of the MDiv students at the time were. Also, I was from a small college in the Midwest, and very few of my classmates had ever heard of it. Early on, though, I discovered that I was not alone. Many of the students came from small midwestern colleges with religious affiliations—St. Olaf, Wheaton, Luther, Bethel, Augustana, and Macalester, to name a few. But there were also some who had graduated from Ivy League universities.

One of my friends on the third floor of Alexander Hall graduated from the Lawrenceville School, one of the oldest prep schools in the country, and then Brown University. Larry Jones wore Brooks Brothers shirts and had a wool sport coat with leather elbow patches. At the beginning I figured he was "old money," though I had no idea what that meant. I'm still not sure if Larry is "old money" because after a few weeks it didn't matter. He became a lifelong friend, along with his roommate Steve Lytch.

The student body was diverse in other ways. Another one of my classmates was studying to become a Unitarian pastor. He often played the cello in his room on the first floor and was an interesting and likeable person. I had been raised to be suspicious of Unitarians because, as I understood it, they lacked any core beliefs. (A popular joke from my childhood: What do you get when you cross a Unitarian with a Jehovah's Witness? Answer: Someone who knocks on doors for no particular reason.) But I liked Jonathan Carey and discovered early on that there was a great deal I could learn from him. He turned out to have many core beliefs and could argue them impressively.

Still another one of my classmates had just been released from prison. Jeb Stuart Magruder had been deputy director of Richard Nixon's 1972 reelection campaign, and he participated in the Watergate cover-up. He cooperated with prosecutors and pled guilty to one felony count of conspiracy to obstruct justice, for which he served seven months in a federal prison. He was the only classmate who bought a house in Princeton for his three years of study. I should have tried harder to get to know him, but in my defense he seemed to spend as little time on campus as possible.

The seminary had a large international student population, and I regret how little effort I made to get to know them. The white students from religiously affiliated colleges in the Midwest seemed to eat all their meals together, while students who came from more than two dozen other countries also ate together—at other tables. What they had in common, I suppose, was that English for them was a second language.

I did make an effort to get to know one of the international students. Her name was Nantawan Boonprasat, a PhD student from Thailand. I invited her to go with me to a major league baseball game. I'm still not sure whether or not this was a date, but whatever it was, it was a bad idea. Yankee Stadium on a weeknight was not a friendly place. We sat in a section with lots of beer drinking, cigar smoking, and umpire cursing. We left before the game was over. I doubt that Nantawan had any further interest in American baseball after that night. She certainly had no further interest in me.

SOCIAL LIFE WITHIN THE STUDENT BODY CONSISTED mostly of drinking beer at a few local establishments. The Rusty Scupper had a Friday afternoon happy hour that was popular. The Annex on Nassau Street was always a good choice for laughter and loud conversation. And then, on weeknights, after studying, there was a place on the university campus we called "the old library." I was never sure who owned and operated it, but it was always filled with students drinking beer by the pitcher. Former faculty members and administrators have told me about a "culture of alcohol" at the seminary that extended beyond the student body. I wasn't aware of how pervasive this culture was at the time, but alcohol was certainly one of the rites of initiation in my seminary education.

The university campus offered lots of foreign-language films on the weekends, and in the days before streaming services seeing them seemed like a treat. My most vivid memory of watching movies with Princeton undergraduates is that they would laugh at dialogue *before* the subtitles appeared, indicating that they got the joke in French, Italian, German, or whatever the language was.

I discovered early on that taking a bus from Princeton to Port Authority in New York City cost only a few dollars, so several times, always on Saturdays, when I should have been studying Hebrew vocabulary, I took the bus to New York, walked around midtown, and window-shopped for hours. I don't remember that I ever bought anything, but I do remember being a wide-eyed tourist.

My field education on Wednesday afternoons and evenings occurred in Philadelphia at the Holmesburg Prison, a frightening old maximum-security prison that was decommissioned in 1995. As part of my orientation there, I was booked and fingerprinted at a Philadelphia police precinct and then brought into the prison by bus, the way a new inmate might experience booking and incarceration. My fellow student chaplains and I ate our meals in the prison dining hall along with the inmates. I even played basketball with the inmates one night, and soon after my first rebound I received an intentional elbow to the jaw, causing a bloody lip. The clear but unspoken message was that, even though I'm tall, I should not attempt to get every rebound.

In 1976 the United States celebrated its bicentennial, and I took an upper-level church history course called "Religion and the American Revolution," taught by John Mulder. John had just received his PhD from Princeton University in American church history and was a popular junior faculty member at the seminary. One Saturday morning

John took the class on a tour of pre-Revolutionary War churches in Philadelphia. The tour—and John's commentary—remain a fond and vivid memory of my seminary experience.

To give a sense of how these relationships work, the privilege of white men not so long ago, I discovered that John had graduated from Hope College and that he had edited the *Anchor*, the weekly student newspaper. So, naturally, I proudly introduced myself as a graduate of Calvin College, Hope's archrival in western Michigan. I also mentioned that I had been associate editor of the *Chimes*, Calvin's weekly student newspaper. Four years later, it was John who made the necessary introduction for me to become editor of the *General Assembly News*, a position he had held for several years before I inherited the job. I was the editor for ten years and became involved in church politics at the national level.

Coursework at the seminary was challenging, though not overwhelming. Introductory courses in Old Testament, New Testament, theology, and church history were required for incoming MDiv students, and the lecture halls for these courses always contained more than two hundred students, which I thought was impressive. Discussion was difficult in these settings, and so in addition to the three lectures per week there were also smaller discussion groups, or precepts, usually led by PhD students.

More than once, after a lecture, I had to walk back to my room in Alexander Hall to think further about what I had heard. Once or twice I walked back in a cold sweat. I decided that in many ways seminary had to be more difficult than law school, because seminary learning occurred on multiple levels. There was always content to be mastered, of course, but there was a further level of belief and conviction. Much of what I had been taught by well-meaning Sunday school teachers along the way had to be rethought and reconsidered. I had to start thinking of the biblical text in some grown-up ways.

One of my Old Testament professors, Bernhard Anderson, referred us one day to Exodus 12:37. The verse claims that "six hundred thousand men on foot"—that is, men of military age, twenty years and older—left Egypt by crossing the Red Sea, the event we now think of as "the exodus." This means, he told us, that if we add women, children, teenagers, and old men, the total number of those who left Egypt would come to over two million people. A column of this size, he said, marching single file, would have extended from Egypt to Sinai and back.

Worse, at least in terms of the historicity of the account, the ancient Egyptians were meticulous record keepers, and there is no archaeological record of any group—let alone one of this size—leaving Egypt. So, clearly, he said, the idea of a mass exodus from Egypt must be "a later exaggeration." Either the exodus never occurred, or the group that left Egypt was significantly smaller than the biblical account suggests.

I seem to recall that he also went into some detail about how much food and water a group of this size would require for its journey, but the point is that most of us had never considered information like this before. We had accepted the story at face value, the way our Sunday school teachers had presented it. A few of my classmates wanted to argue, but that seemed like a waste of time to me. What I had to do, and what I spent a considerable amount of time doing (when I wasn't drinking pitchers of beer with my classmates) was to decide what was left. If the faith that I learned from my Sunday school teachers could be so easily challenged, what was left for me to claim?

Like the majority of my classmates, I was able to sort most of this out before I graduated. Most of us, I believe, graduated with a sturdier, more robust faith than the one we arrived with. But there have been times through the years when I have been faced with similar challenges requiring further reflection.

Long after graduation, I remember reading a book about Jesus by John Dominic Crossan that left me unsettled for several days. I knew about Crossan and his frequent collaborator Marcus Borg. I was also familiar with the work of the Jesus Seminar. But for some reason this particular book by Crossan got under my skin in a way that these issues hadn't for many years. Was it true, as Crossan claimed, that Jesus's body was more than likely eaten by wild dogs? Was it true, then, that there was no such thing as a physical, bodily resurrection? These questions were close to the center of my faith. But my seminary classes had taught me how to think theologically, how to navigate my way through most challenges. And eventually I navigated my way through this one.

ONE OF THE BELIEFS THAT I BROUGHT with me to seminary concerned the church's stance toward same-sex relationships. Even the phrase "the church's stance" irritates me now, because it suggests that the church speaks with one voice on every subject.

The church in which I had been raised, the Christian Reformed Church, had a stance on same-sex matters, and I'm surprised now that I accepted it without much thought. The stance was that Christian homosexuals must be wholeheartedly received by the church—in other words, into membership—but that homosexual acts themselves must be condemned. This was the vocabulary in use at the time, and it's remarkable to me that this particular stance seemed enlightened and generous.

As an editor of the student newspaper, I covered what happened at the Synod meeting where this stance was adopted, and I interviewed the pastor, Leonard Greenway, who moderated the debate. The paper devoted an entire page to the subject in its September 21, 1973, edition, and my byline is at the top of the page. After much discussion—"a fine brotherly spirit was exhibited," although there were "a few moments of unpleasantness"—it was decided that homosexuality is an acquired characteristic and therefore something for which an individual is responsible. In other words, though no one used this vocabulary then, to be gay was not merely a choice, but a sinful choice.

It didn't occur to me to question any of this, even though I had questioned other stances the church had taken—the stance regarding war, for example. That subject got my attention because I came close to being drafted before the Vietnam War finally came to an end. With the church's stance on same-sex relationships, though, I thought I had no direct interest. I did not know anyone who was gay. I discovered later that, as a matter of fact, I knew several people who were gay, men I had gone to school with over the years. But not many people at the time dared to reveal a same-sex preference, so the subject was for me mainly an abstraction. That is, until I arrived at seminary.

Princeton Seminary opened my eyes not only to new ways of understanding the exodus, but also to pressing social and cultural issues. In the early 1970s, the Presbyterian church had adopted language that was not so different from the stance of the Christian Reformed Church. Avowed, practicing homosexuals (once again, the accepted vocabulary) were not permitted to be ordained in the Presbyterian church because such an act would be contrary to the church's "charter and calling." The vote on the floor of the General Assembly was six hundred to fifty. Not even close.

By the time I arrived at Princeton, the subject was, not surprisingly, being discussed and debated. A "gay caucus" was established on campus, and fifteen of my classmates publicly aligned themselves with the cause. A *New York Times* reporter covering the development estimated that if fifteen students went public with their sexual preference, there might be as many as fifty students in the student body (of eight hundred) with a same-sex preference. I'm not sure how the reporter arrived at this number, but it was startling at the time. So many gay and lesbian students at a school preparing young people for ministry! And, of course, it contributed to the reputation Princeton had for being more liberal than, say, Fuller.

I studied the relatively few biblical texts that refer to this subject, I listened to my classmates, especially the ones who had dared to announce their sexual preferences, often risking their chances at ordination by doing so, and I gradually came to my own stance on the subject. By the time I graduated my stance was set and hasn't wavered in the years since. My stance was that gays and lesbians should be welcomed fully and without condition into the Christian church and that ordination should be open to them.

What I regret all these years later is not having used my voice or my position to advocate for my brothers and sisters who were gay and lesbian. Most people who knew me, including members of the churches I served, knew my stance, but I was far from outspoken. I had my reasons, of course, for being quiet. I continued to believe, for example, that the church should be a big tent with lots of stances and viewpoints. But I should have done more to challenge those who did not agree with me. Without a challenge, they were unlikely to grow and evolve, as I had been pushed to grow and evolve in my own understanding. I believe that those with a voice are compelled to use it for those who have no voice.

OUTSIDE THE SEMINARY DINING HALL ARE SEVERAL plaques honoring graduates of the seminary who were martyred in the course of their work because of what they believed. I passed these plaques every day, three times each day, for two years. I noticed them early on, and I read their contents, but over time they lost some of their impact. Even so, I knew they were there and what they stood for. So did my classmates.

One of the plaques honors Elijah Parish Lovejoy, a Presbyterian pastor, journalist, newspaper editor, and abolitionist. I made a special note about Lovejoy because of his interest in writing and publishing. Lovejoy was editor of the *St. Louis Observer*, a Presbyterian weekly, in which he strongly condemned slavery and supported gradual emancipation. Missouri was a slave state, and Lovejoy's views were not popular. In 1835 a letter signed by prominent citizens in St. Louis asked him to moderate the tone of his editorials. In response Lovejoy doubled down on his views, as well as his right to publish them.

Two years later, after moving to Alton, Illinois, nominally a free state, Lovejoy was attacked again, dragged to the street, shot, and killed one night by a proslavery mob that had attempted to destroy Lovejoy's printing press and abolitionist literature. There was such fear surrounding the issue at the time of Lovejoy's death that no funeral service was held. The town newspaper did not report his death, and he was buried in an unmarked grave. Other newspapers around the country did report on the murder, however, and over the years Lovejoy has become a symbol of courage, someone who was willing to die for what he believed. So, in addition to wealth and alcohol, the seminary also introduced me to the idea of martyrdom.

I realize now, though, to my regret, that I was no Elijah Parish Lovejoy.

6

That's What They Call Grace

For grace to be grace, it must give us things we didn't know we needed and take us places where we didn't know we didn't want to go. As we stumble through the crazily altered landscape of our lives, we find that God is enjoying our attention as never before.

Kathleen Norris, *Acedia & Me:*
A Marriage, Monks, and a Writer's Life

For me, becoming isn't about arriving somewhere or achieving a certain aim. I see it instead as forward motion, a means of evolving, a way to reach continuously toward a better self. The journey doesn't end.

Michelle Obama, *Becoming*

My first attempt at preaching a sermon to churchpeople, as opposed to seminary classmates, did not go well.

I forget what I preached about, but then it was a forgettable sermon. It's not that I didn't put time and effort into it. I even asked my wife to sit and listen to it on Saturday afternoon as I stood in the living room of our first apartment in Iowa City and read the thing to her. She was encouraging, but she must also have been terrified that this would become a weekly routine in our marriage.

Public speaking was something I had always dreaded. I took the required undergraduate course in public speaking during the summer so that fewer of my friends would be around to witness the spectacle. It was awful. Standing in front of any group of people, even the six or seven who took the summer course in college, was anxiety-producing. I would sweat, tremble visibly, and speak far too softly for anyone to make out exactly what I was saying.

I have mentioned this to people over the years, and they find it hard to believe because I eventually pushed myself to become what might generously be described as an adequate public speaker. But the story is true. I was always scared to speak publicly, and early on that fear was nearly debilitating.

For my very first sermon at the church in Iowa City, I wore the only suit I owned, a tan corduroy, three-piece number with wide lapels, which I must have liked when I saw it on the rack. On me the suit was humorously ill-fitting, even though the store tailor had done his best to accommodate my tall, thin frame. My presentation was awkward, and that was before I opened my mouth.

I carried my typewritten manuscript to the pulpit, and my hands trembled noticeably as I walked. I was pale and sweaty, and I'm sure the people in the front pews wondered if I would be sick. I read the entire thing in about seven minutes without glancing up once from the typewritten page. It would be years before I made my first unplanned gesture. And then I hurried back to my seat, relieved to be finished.

Years later I spoke with Bill Nibbelink, the person who was assigned to be my mentor at the Iowa City church, and he says that he considered raising his hand at that point and calling out, "Doug, read it again! We might have missed something the first time!" But no one, as I recall, said anything. Instead they sat in stunned silence. The most gracious response that day would have been that I needed a great deal of work. A more sober analysis would be that I showed very little potential for a career as a preacher.

Within a couple months, the pastor at the Iowa City church, Al Helder, who was supposed to be my mentor for the year, accepted a call to a church in Colorado where he could be closer to the mountains and to skiing. I have always wondered if his decision had something to do with me and how much time I was going to require from him. Christmas was coming up in a few weeks, and the church budget couldn't support an interim pastor, so the elders approached me and asked me to take on the responsibility for preaching most Sundays, beginning with Christmas morning and continuing for the next seven months. I think we all knew what a difficult decision this was, but they had little choice. They were stuck with me and determined to make the best of the choices they had. They appointed a member of the church council to be my mentor, and he agreed to meet with me on Monday mornings in his office at the university.

Those Monday morning meetings in Bill's office were the high point of my year in Iowa City. Bill was a professor of early childhood development, and his office walls were decorated with dozens of drawings by children. Our conversations often ranged far from church matters, but Bill always managed to say to me what needed to be said. He also coached me to do some of the wildest and most imaginative children's sermons that the church had ever witnessed, including one that involved his dog, though I now forget the point of that particular one. Looking back, it seems clear to me that those children's sermons were mainly for me. They helped me to relax and be more natural at the front of the church. And, miraculously, I was. I also loved the laughter.

For my end-of-year evaluation, Bill took me on his motorboat for a cruise on Coralville Lake, a nearby reservoir. At some point on the cruise, he shut off the engine and handed me the written assessment of the year for my approval and signature. I read it in the back of the boat. I still have it. It's a model of how to speak the truth to people like me. Bill noted some of the areas where I seemed to do well (his older daughter, for example, thought I was "hilarious" in my leadership of the senior high Sunday school class, which she meant as high praise), but he also wrote plainly about my chief weakness, which continued to be my preaching. It was the word "pitiful" that I have never forgotten. That was Bill's description of my speaking style when I first arrived at the church. No sugar coating. He was right. And it's in my permanent record.

I might have quit at that point and gone to law school, but something about Bill's directness—and his belief that I could be better than I was—convinced me to keep working at it. He saw something in me that I had not dared to imagine in myself.

PART OF THE PROBLEM WITH MY PREACHING, I now see, is that I thought of myself as a writer. I loved the way my words looked on the page, which is hardly ever a recipe for great public speaking.

I became a writer in fifth grade, which is well before I became a speaker. Early on in my life I remember wanting to be good at something, but the "something" I had in mind was always sports. What I wanted, more than anything, was to be a major league baseball player, preferably for the Detroit Tigers, and I devoted hours and hours to achieving this goal. I certainly had the size for it. Sadly, though, I never really had the ability to play any sport particularly well, and desire alone cannot overcome a lack of ability.

My mother wanted me to be a concert pianist, or at least good enough to sit down at the piano and pound out an old hymn. So I went to my lessons each week for a couple of years and then practiced at home for the required one hour per day, but my heart was never in it. The teacher finally told my mother that she would gladly keep taking her money, but that the lessons weren't going anywhere. My mother, now in her nineties, still remembers this conversation with sadness. I did not inherit the family piano.

Because of my size—and maybe my lack of speed—I was always the catcher on my Little League baseball teams. I liked to make runners think twice about trying to score. I dared them to cross home plate. I couldn't hit for beans, though, maybe because of my near-sightedness. Little League is filled with decent fielders and poor hitters, and I was one of them. During my freshman year in high school, I was cut from the baseball team during the spring tryouts, and I never played baseball again, a rejection that still produces a twinge of resentment.

I did play high school football. Any two-hundred-pounder, which I was if you included the helmet and pads and rounded up a little, had a pretty good chance of making the team and playing the line. I enjoyed the physical part of the game, and on the defensive line I threw myself at quarterbacks, running backs, and anyone who happened to be near me. Good vision is not required to play the line in high school football, nor is a lot of skill. Our team, sadly, was not very good. Our record my senior year was three wins and five losses, and when the season was over, my athletic career came to a desultory end. I retired my game jersey by taking it home after the last game and not telling anyone.

Happily, though, my fifth-grade teacher, Mrs. DeJong, saw something in me that was not related to sports. One day she assigned an essay to my class with the prompt "my most embarrassing moment," and my essay turned out to be a winner. Mrs. DeJong encouraged me to enter my essay in the annual all-school "prose and poetry" competition. I might have hesitated if I had known ahead of time that the winners would be expected to read their entries at an all-school assembly. But I entered and learned a few weeks later that I had won second prize.

The first-prize winner was Randy Vander Mey, a sixth grader who wrote a futuristic short story. I didn't know at the time that just anybody was allowed to write something in the genre of science fiction, so I was impressed by Randy's imagination. And when I heard him read his entry at the all-school assembly, I was impressed again. It was really good. Instead of feeling bad about my second-place finish, what I remember thinking was that I was right up there with a sixth grader (who now teaches English literature at a university in southern California).

My essay, sadly, doesn't exist anymore, which is surprising for something that has turned out to be so important to me. My mother saved so much from my childhood, including a lock of hair from my first haircut and all of my grade school report cards, that this seems like an odd omission. Maybe she wasn't as proud of it as I was. What I wrote about was going to the high-end children's clothing store, Clements Young Ages, where my mother liked to shop for me. I was in the dressing room one day, in my underwear, waiting for my mother to hand me something in a larger size. The next person to pull back the curtain, however, was not my mother, but a young girl about my age, and I was embarrassed to be seen by her. That was the entire story.

Without having the essay in front of me, I'm guessing that what was good about it was the wrenching honesty and dark humor. Already at eleven years old I was finding my voice. Mrs. DeJong had done her job. She let me know that I was good at something. I could string a few words together in a way that made people laugh and (I would learn later) that could make people cry. To me, at the time, this felt like discovering a superpower. I had no idea what I was going to do with it. But at age eleven I knew I had it.

I STILL LIKE THE LOOK OF MY WORDS on a page. And, for that reason, I will never be much of a public speaker. I wouldn't recommend my method of sermon preparation to any new preacher. On the other hand, I did learn, over the years, to speak my words aloud as I typed them. And so I adopted a kind of hybrid speaking-writing style. Speaking didn't improve my writing, but my writing probably made my sermons worth listening to. At least that's what I told myself for forty years.

Mostly, when I write, I write to figure things out. I wouldn't know what I believed about a biblical text, for example, until I had written my sermon. I would get to the end and be startled by my conclusion. I grew in faith during my year in Iowa City because every week I found myself sitting in front of a typewriter and declaring all sorts of truths that I never expected to say aloud.

The underlying principle is fairly simple. If a child is having a hard time expressing himself, you hand him a crayon and a sheet of paper. And then you say, "Draw me a picture of how you're feeling." In my experience children can often express themselves eloquently when they draw whatever it is they can't say aloud. For me the act of writing allowed me to express what would never have come out of my mouth.

ONE SUNDAY NIGHT IN IOWA CITY—I was responsible for both morning and evening services—I preached a sermon based on the parable of the prodigal son. For reasons that only seem obvious to me now, I returned to this particular story several times in Iowa City. One time I preached from the perspective of the loving father, another time from the perspective of the older brother, and still another time from the perspective of the younger brother, the prodigal. I don't remember which angle I was taking at this evening service, but at some point during the sermon I remember that I began to cry.

I have seen other preachers continue to preach while crying, which has always impressed me, but I have never been able to do it.

I have only cried one or two other times during my entire career as a preacher, and each time I found that I had to stop speaking. That's what I did this evening. I stared at my manuscript, with tears running down my cheeks, for what seemed like several minutes.

My sermon, as I recall, wasn't particularly emotional. I have often been surprised over the years when people would tell me that something I said in a sermon made them cry. I never try to make anyone cry, and I would find it manipulative if someone did it to me. What produced tears on this occasion wasn't anything I had written, but a sudden recognition of something. I had been talking that night about grace, a word I thought I knew well. What the parable teaches, I remember saying, is God's confounding unconditional love. And those words, or words like them, suddenly did me in. I couldn't go on. I knew the concept. I knew what grace was. But I had never really experienced the exact meaning of the word before this night.

Ming Tsaung, a psychiatrist at the university hospital, was sitting in the front row, and I remember that he was watching me carefully, maybe wondering if I was having an episode he would be required to treat. The tears soon stopped, and I was able to go on with my sermon.

The next morning, in Bill's office, he and I talked about what had happened. He seemed pleased, which surprised me. He seemed to sense that, in my preaching, I was beginning to find the connection between my head and my heart, that I was beginning to express what was in my heart. Grace had been little more than an abstraction for much of my life, and suddenly, in the twenty-fourth year of my life, grace started to become a reality.

Let me put this reality as simply as I can: the good people at that church in Iowa City loved me. I figured they probably wouldn't because I wasn't very good at being their pastor. I turned out to be worse at preaching than I was at hitting a baseball. But they surprised me by loving me anyway. Love, I discovered, is not always transactional. And what's even more amazing is that those people continued to show up week after week. If there had been a drop-off in attendance, I would have heard about it. Instead, they gave me the best gift it is possible to give a preacher: they listened to me. (I should note that they didn't have to pay my salary, which must have helped a little, but still.)

My wife loved me too, during that first year of marriage, even though I realized early on that I wasn't always loveable. She sat and listened to several more sermons on Saturday afternoons and always offered generous words of encouragement. And she never said what she must have been thinking: "Have you ever thought about using your gifts in another field?"

Somehow, because of those two things, I was able to make the connection that this is what God's love for us must feel like. Undeserved. Unearned. Free in a way you wouldn't expect anything so good to be free. And overwhelming enough that, when you first realize what it is, you have to stop and cry and think about this thing you have discovered, knowing that your life will never be the same because of it.

Lots of writers over the years have expressed themselves eloquently about grace, which means that lots of writers, like me, needed to experience grace at some point in their lives. One of my favorite descriptions of grace comes from Frederick Buechner, whom I used to envy from a distance because he was both a Presbyterian pastor and a writer. "Grace," he wrote, "is something you can never get but can only be given. There's no way to earn it or deserve it or bring it about, any more than you can deserve the taste of raspberries and cream or earn good looks. A good night's sleep is grace and so are good dreams. Most tears are grace. The smell of rain is grace. Somebody loving you is grace."

I was loved. I was sure of it. And my tears that Sunday night in Iowa City were grace. Bill explaining to me what happened the next day in his office covered in drawings by children was grace. I had never felt anything so wonderful in my life, and I was changed because of it. Not all at once, of course, but a change began in me that I wanted and needed and welcomed.

The first and most obvious change was that I stopped telling people I was looking forward to a career in publishing or maybe editorial work. I heard myself saying for the first time that I was moving toward ordination, that I felt called to be a pastor. Anyone who has ever experienced grace, anyone who can name it, wants to point it out and talk about it. Without anyone telling me, I knew that my work as a pastor would be to say, "Look! Can you see that? That's what they call grace. Isn't it something?"

The Boat Is Leaking

Sometimes the best thing we can do for each other is to talk honestly about being wrong.

Nadia Bolz-Weber, *Pastrix: The Cranky,*
Beautiful Faith of a Sinner & Saint

I know now that we never get over great losses; we absorb them, and they carve us into different, often kinder, creatures.

Gail Caldwell, *Let's Take the Long Way Home:*
A Memoir of Friendship

My father once told me that I did everything "the hard way."

I want to believe that he was giving me an insight into myself, a helpful framework for understanding my decisions and choices to that point in my life. But I thought then, as I do now, that his words were most likely spoken out of exasperation. What I heard him say was that he was throwing in the towel and giving up. I was not the son he had expected. I kept surprising him, and not in good ways, leading to long stretches of silence and estrangement in my adult life.

As he saw it, he had done everything a father was expected to do. He had provided for me and had given me the best that he was able to give, which was true in a material sense. For example, he had "put a roof over my head," as he reminded me more than once. He had also loved my mother throughout a marriage of nearly seventy years, which is no small thing. Beyond that, he had provided me with an education that had not been available to him when he was growing up. To a man of his generation, to a man who always wanted to do the right thing, he had done enough. In fact, as he saw it, *more* than enough.

And yet, to his mind, I was not catching on. I could have chosen the easier way, which I take to mean the way he had followed with his own life—not venturing far from home, not leaving the church in which he had been raised, not breaking all of the unwritten rules of life—but instead I chose another way, my way, and to him that was next to impossible to comprehend. After a certain point, he decided not to try.

My father did not go to college. When he graduated from high school, World War II was not yet at an end, and so he did what nearly all young men were doing at the time. He enlisted. I'm pretty sure he would not have gone to college if there had been no war. His father hadn't gone. And neither had his grandparents. They were immigrants to this country from the Netherlands. They worked hard, grateful to have work to do, and along the way, they knew extraordinary hardship, including the deaths of two daughters. To have survived, to have made the transition from one continent to another, to have learned a new language and adapted to a new culture, was enough. College was for a future generation. And that generation, as it turned out, was mine.

I learned much later in my life that my father had been accepted, after the war ended, at the School of the Art Institute of Chicago, a choice that was available to him because of both the GI Bill and his extraordinary drawing ability. But because of the large number of men returning from military service, his admission had been delayed by one semester, from September to January. And it was during those few months that he met my mother and started dating her. Instead of enrolling at SAIC, he married my mother the following June and went to work as a commercial artist, an entry-level position at the Jaqua Advertising Agency, where eventually he became president and chairman of the board. His lack of a college degree was an obstacle he had overcome. And then some.

Throughout his life, interestingly, he took a dim view of artists who went to art school. They would apply for a job in advertising at Jaqua, they would display the portfolios they had put together in art school, and later, at home, my father would shake his head and describe their efforts as amateurish. He had learned to draw the right way, he said, not with a "so-called professor" looking over his shoulder, but with a deadline, "with real money at stake." I heard these stories many times, and I grew up thinking that art school was the worst choice an aspiring artist could possibly make. And then I learned about my father's decision not to pursue a degree, not to leave home for Chicago, and I felt new sympathy for those art school graduates who over the years sat in my father's office proudly displaying their work. I suppose they were doing things "the hard way" too.

I did not enlist at age eighteen, or set off for the war in the Pacific, not knowing if I would ever return. It's entirely possible, if I had gone to war and then returned, that I would not have wanted to leave home again, a few months later, for Chicago, to pursue a degree in art. I was also not an only child, as my father was, and so I never felt a particular need to take care of my parents in their old age. My father had good reasons for the choices he made. In similar circumstances, I might have made the same choices. On the other hand, I had good reasons for the choices I did make and for breaking lots of unwritten rules along the way. I look back and feel proud of what I did and how I did it. If I did everything "the hard way," as he saw it, then okay. It was my way. And some of it *was* hard.

After my experience of grace in Iowa City, and my year of work there as a student pastor, I returned to Princeton with both vocational clarity and a new marriage. To my surprise, no one cared much about my newfound vocational clarity, but my new marital status was of interest. It meant that I had lost my on-campus living privileges. I would no longer be living on the third floor of Alexander Hall, where I had enjoyed all those leisurely Sunday mornings under the influence of coffee, the Sunday *New York Times*, and magical thinking (about what I was doing at seminary). Instead, my wife and I found an apartment closer to the law school where she had been accepted, and I became a commuter student for the third and final year of my MDiv degree. The friends I had made in my first and second years of seminary had graduated and moved on.

In yet another example of magical thinking, I thought that I could return to the denomination of my childhood and seek ordination there, but I soon learned that the decision to attend Princeton, rather than the denominational seminary closer to home, had irrevocably closed that door. After a brief, painful, and ultimately unsuccessful attempt to reconnect with the Christian Reformed Church at the beginning of my third year of seminary, I made the difficult decision to become a Presbyterian. My father described this at the time as an example of doing things "the hard way," and I won't lie: that decision was as hard as any I have ever made. It threw me into a hole of depression that I didn't climb out of for at least a year.

When the door to ordination in the Christian Reformed Church closed, I made an appointment with Arthur Adams, the academic dean at Princeton, and told him of my plan to become a Presbyterian and to seek ordination in the Presbyterian Church. I had been told that any student who wanted to change denominations and become a Presbyterian would have to get his blessing.

At one point in our conversation, he told me to "stop apologizing" for not having grown up in the Presbyterian Church. "Everyone in the Presbyterian Church comes from somewhere else," he said, which turned out to be true in the churches I served. "Cradle Presbyterians," I soon learned, were rare. When I expressed concern about what was then an oversupply of Presbyterian pastors, the dean assured me that "there is always room for an exceptional pastor." It wasn't until the drive home that I recognized his careful choice of words. He did not say there would always be room for me. I assumed, on the basis of scant evidence, that I would be an exceptional pastor, which is what I set out to be. In addition to my inclination to break unwritten rules and defy parental authority, I also had an "I'll show you" attitude. I was determined to make this new denominational relationship a success.

The Presbyterian Church—known then as the United Presbyterian Church in the United States of America—welcomed me with open arms, which surprised me and turned out to be another experience of grace. Not immediately, but over time, I began to recognize that becoming a Presbyterian was the best decision I could have made, in many ways a far better fit for me. Still, I had left my family, my hometown, and the church of my childhood behind. None of this was easy.

The process leading to ordination in the Presbyterian Church is long and complicated, involving a series of exams, some psychological testing, and many, many meetings with various committees.

I told my story about preaching on the parable of the prodigal son and recognizing grace for the first time until I became quite good at it. I even worried that in the constant retelling it was losing some of its authenticity. The last step in the process is an exam by the presbytery that has monitored the entire process, and though I didn't exactly shine in my answers that night, I didn't stumble badly enough to be thrown out.

The question that nearly did me in involved the issue of "fencing the table." The Christian Reformed Church, like the old Presbyterian Church in Scotland, has certain rules and restrictions about who is invited to participate in the Lord's Supper. Not just anyone can walk up and have a bite to eat.

The Presbyterian Church today, in a break with its Scottish past, places few restrictions on participation. Baptized children, for example, are always welcome at the table, even without the benefit of a confirmation class, though parents are encouraged to explain the meaning of the meal to them. The subtleties were lost on me at the time, however, and I wasn't terribly articulate in my response. In the end, though, they voted to take a chance on me. I was approved for ordination, and after the vote there was polite applause when I walked back into the room where the exam had been held. A few of them must have been thinking, "Enjoy it, kid. It might be the last time church-people clap their hands for you."

I OFTEN USE THE WORDS "career" and "vocation" interchangeably, as though they're the same thing. They're not, of course. And my best guess as to why I do this is that I was raised and socialized in a culture that emphasized—for men, at least—the surpassing importance of having a career. But I was also raised in a Dutch Calvinist subculture, a sect, that prided itself on seeing the world and individual lives in theological terms.

Thinking of my life's work as vocation, though, is a happier way for me to reflect on it. I mostly enjoyed the sense of calling and purpose with which I began my work. Becoming a Minister of Word and Sacrament in the Presbyterian Church, however, was a poor career choice. What I had learned from my father and grandfather about hard work and ambition, plus my "I'll show you" attitude, did not serve me well in my career as a pastor.

The 1950s, my early childhood years, were arguably the high point of mainline denominational life in the United States. Churches grew, and then they planted new churches. Pastors may have been poorly paid at the time, but they nevertheless enjoyed a high degree of social esteem. Seminaries enjoyed record numbers of students, and the established seminaries were able to grow their endowments to astonishing levels. (I remember James I. McCord, president of Princeton Theological Seminary when I was an MDiv student, joking in an informal meeting with wide-eyed students that "the first $100 million is always the hardest to raise.") Many major denominations at the time had their headquarters in New York City, at 475 Riverside Drive, and this prestigious address seemed like confirmation to me that these churches were firmly established within American culture. Getting a job with the Presbyterian Church, I thought, would be like getting a job with Xerox or IBM.

And it was, in more ways than one. Xerox and IBM may once have been highly regarded, but they have been surpassed by many other companies over the years.

When I was born, my parents bought a house in the suburbs and paid cash for it. They lived in that house for more than forty years, raised their three children there, and saw no reason to move until they downsized to a condominium much later in their lives. The house where I grew up was only a short walk from the church my family attended and a short drive from the company where my father worked.

That church in our neighborhood grew and grew, seemingly without effort. I remember that members had to take turns, once a month, sitting in the church basement, watching the service on closed-circuit television, in order to have enough seating available upstairs. On the first Sunday of the month, for example, everyone with last names beginning A to F would take their turn sitting on folding chairs downstairs. And closed-circuit television was a curious-enough phenomenon that some of us actually enjoyed watching the black-and-white image. I also remember that our church planted other churches farther out, in even newer suburbs. A few families would be assigned to "seed" this new church, and within a couple of years those new churches would be self-sustaining. The church in my childhood was always filled to overflowing on Sundays. This, in my imagination, was the way church was supposed to be.

The 1960s, however, were a turning point in church life, but no one knew just how much of a turning point they would be. By the time I was ordained, in 1980, the signs of change and decline were already clear. The response to change and decline, uncomfortable to acknowledge now, was not to proclaim the gospel in fresh and compelling ways, but to try just about anything to reclaim what once belonged to us.

I remember that Fred Anderson, senior pastor of the church where I was ordained, set a challenging goal for our church of "2,000 by 2000." In other words, we were determined to double our membership over the next twenty years. And so, as the only staff member with the word "evangelism" in my job description, I attended church growth seminars and retooled the church's outreach efforts. I even wrote my doctor of ministry (DMin) thesis about helping church members to speak about their faith in language that was comfortable and natural. All of it, it seems so clear to me now, was nothing more than a desperate struggle to get back on top, which is where we thought we belonged. My work ethic and ambition, my "I'll show you attitude," were easily coopted by this response to decline.

What we didn't know—and to be fair, what we could not have known—was that a beautiful neo-Gothic building, with an expensive pipe organ and traditional music program, across the street from a state capitol building (in a downtown area where there was little to no parking), would not be the magnet for new members we imagined it would be. Our preaching was biblical, our members were friendly, our music was lovely, and our programming was outstanding. But none of that was enough. The world had changed, and the world where Presbyterians were on top and in charge was not coming back.

At one level I knew this was true, but in my determination to be successful I was willing to work all the hours that would be necessary. I put my career ahead of my vocation, and in doing that I ignored what was obvious to everyone else. Slowly at first, and then wholeheartedly, I embraced this other vision of the church—strong, powerful, financially secure, and always growing. I was determined to become the "exceptional pastor" that Arthur Adams told me about. And in many ways I was.

IT SEEMS TO ME NOW that we get so much of our lives wrong. And we almost never get the chance to make what was wrong right again. My relationship with my father was difficult, and it ended unresolved at his death. On three different occasions I started therapy about an issue in my life, usually having to do with my work as a pastor, and each time the therapy came back to that one formative relationship in my life: "Tell me about your relationship with your father," the therapist would say.

While my career as a Presbyterian pastor was sometimes difficult, there were seasons of growth, just as I have many good memories of time spent with my father. During my years at the church in Wheaton, attendance and membership soared, the staff expanded, the building doubled in size, and a parking lot was added. All of that seemed, at the time, like the way things were supposed to be. Mostly, though, the churches I served looked backward rather than forward. They remembered better times, when the pews teemed with young families, when the Sunday school rooms were filled with happy children, and when budgets seemed to raise themselves. I found those days hard, as though I was trying to live up to a standard I could never meet—my father's standard, what he thought of as the easier way, the right way to do things.

I wish I could have had one more conversation with my father, not that it would have changed much, and I sometimes feel the same way about the church. I wish I could go back in time and be the one to say to the elders, "Listen to me. Let's not pay attention to the numbers. Let's keep talking about what we know, which is grace."

Sometimes, when I think about it, I am outraged, and when I am, I find comfort in the psalms of lament:

> Be gracious to me, O LORD, for I am in distress;
>   my eye wastes away from grief,
>   my soul and body also.
> For my life is spent with sorrow,
>   and my years with sighing;
> my strength fails because of my misery,
>   and my bones waste away.
>
> (Ps. 31:9–10)

One reason I like the music of Leonard Cohen is that his lyrics sound like those Old Testament laments. In his song "Everybody Knows," Cohen sings about how everybody knows the captain lied and the boat is sinking, and they all feel broken, like when a loved one dies. It's not a particularly hopeful song, but then laments don't have to be hopeful. Instead, they are unflinching descriptions of the way things are. Cohen's lyrics—sung with a softly played piano and a penetrating violin—are a reminder that what we long for and what we have are often two different things.

I find it interesting that in the mid-1980s, as I started to come to terms with my own career, Cohen considered retiring from songwriting in order to join a monastery. His 1984 album had debuted to a lukewarm reception, and he began to wonder what his life amounted to. He judged the quality of his work by the number of albums he sold, and to himself he was a failure. But vocation, he decided, is not the same as career. For Cohen the call he listened to was the call to write music. He chose "the hard way," as my father would say. And I'm glad he did.

I chose "the hard way" too. I changed denominations two-thirds of the way through my seminary training, I sought ordination in a denomination where few people knew me or understood my background, and I found little support or understanding in all of it from my father, at least none that he ever shared with me. What I wish now is that I could have seen more clearly, early on, what was true— namely, that the Presbyterian boat was leaking, that the seminary lied, and that there was nothing I could do to save it, no matter how many hours I gave. My call was not to sell albums, but, like Cohen, to write music.

The Least Likely People

Never once did Jesus scan the room for the best example of holy living and send that person out to tell others about him. He always sent out stumblers and sinners. I find that comforting.

Nadia Bolz-Weber, *Accidental Saints:*
Finding God in All the Wrong People

We are what we pretend to be, and so we must be careful what we pretend to be.

Kurt Vonnegut, *Mother Night*

When I was ordained to be a Minister of Word and Sacrament on September 20, 1980, one month short of my twenty-seventh birthday, I had little idea who I was or what I was doing. I would never have said this aloud to anyone, but forty years later I can say that, at the beginning, I was pretending to be someone I wasn't, someone I might never become. In my ordination, I was taking on an identity that I would grow into over the course of many years, an identity that still in some ways surprises me.

It was a hot day, one of those awful, last-gasp-of-summer days, when everyone is tired of hot weather and looking forward to fall. The church where I was ordained, the venerable Pine Street Presbyterian Church, was not air-conditioned. It was an old building, and with its neo-Gothic architecture it was designed to look even older than it was. Retrofitting air-conditioning would not have been possible without running ductwork along its gorgeous vaulted ceiling. So, there we were, irritable, sweaty, and complaining, before the first notes from the pipe organ. I can't say that I was excited, even though ordination is the culmination of a great deal of work, more than I ever imagined. Mostly I was relieved. I wanted to get through it with no one raising a hand and asking if what we were doing was such a good idea.

My parents were there for the occasion, as they had been for all the important occasions of my life, including graduations and piano recitals and Little League baseball games. One of my favorite college professors, Richard Mouw, was there to preach the sermon, trying one more time to point me in the right direction. And fifteen, or maybe it was twenty, of my new colleagues in the Presbytery of Carlisle, most of whom I barely knew, were there too, all wearing black pulpit robes in the sweltering heat.

Instead of keeping the service short, which I'm sure everyone would have welcomed, we made the thing as long as we could, with a full ordination liturgy. "Everything but a baptism," my senior pastor, Fred Anderson, proudly said, implying that he was still looking around until the last minute for a baby to baptize.

In addition to the sermon, there were two long charges, one to the candidate—me—and another to the congregation. (In his charge to the congregation, Fred warned church members to be on their best behavior because pastors are most likely to quit during their first five years after ordination, and as I listened to Fred I wondered if I would last more than a few months.) We celebrated communion, though I had argued that it wasn't absolutely essential at an ordination service. I remember standing behind the table for the first time, handling the elements, and speaking the words that I had committed to memory during the previous week. I was too afraid of making a mistake to be present in the moment, though I remember filling the silver chalice and, with a sense of wonder, lifting it for the first time.

During the ancient ordination rite—the laying on of hands— I knelt on the chancel steps and was surrounded by a mob of clergy and elders, including my father, who solemnly laid their hands on me and welcomed me to an apostolic tradition that includes everyone from the apostle Peter to my childhood pastor, and now, I realized, to me. I wanted to feel something mystical in that moment, but mostly what I felt was the weight of those hands. I can feel the weight of them now.

No one, as far as I know, said aloud that day that I was obviously a fraud, although I must have looked like one, a tall, skinny kid, with an ill-fitting clerical collar. No one laughed as the ordination questions were asked, and I still wonder why not.

"Will you in your own life seek to follow the Lord Jesus Christ, love your neighbors, and work for the reconciliation of the world?"

"Will you pray for and seek to serve the people with energy, intelligence, imagination, and love?"

"Do you promise to further the peace, unity, and purity of the church?"

I knew the expected answers to these and all the other ordination questions, and I knew how I would answer them before they were asked. But listening to them in that moment, I couldn't help but hear the absurdity in them. I wanted to turn around and say with a shrug, "You must be kidding, right?" Instead, I faced forward, answered aloud, and assumed that I would soon be exposed. No one has ever been more of a pretender in that moment than I was.

I AM TEMPTED TO CHALK UP MY FEELINGS that day to "imposter syndrome," which is not (yet) considered a psychological disorder but is indeed a widespread phenomenon, especially among high-achieving and successful women. According to the studies I have read, some people, especially perfectionists, experience in their work an overwhelming sense of inadequacy or chronic self-doubt, as though all that has been achieved is a result of luck, say, and not hard work. So these people live in fear of being unmasked, exposed, or found out.

It's not as though I've never experienced the feeling of inadequacy or a regular twinge of self-doubt, but what I wondered then, as I do now, was whether *anyone* is up to the job of being a pastor.

I had this same thought, as a matter of fact, already on my first day of seminary classes. One of my classmates—I will never forget this—showed up in class wearing a clerical collar. I thought he looked pretty good in it too, polished and ready, in a way that most of the rest of us in class that day did not. He was certain about who he was, or pretended to be, while I was just trying to figure out what in the world I was doing there.

Instead of wearing my ordination confidently, as though I had earned it and was therefore ready, however, I wore it awkwardly at first. Then, over time, I began to lose myself in it, so that after my retirement I had to look hard for a self that was distinct from the ordained person I had become.

A LITTLE-KNOWN TRUTH AMONG PASTORS, a kind of trade secret, is that congregations, the people we have come to serve, teach us how to be pastors. We think we have learned the trade by watching others do it, or by taking a few classes in what is laughably called "practical theology," but the truth is that churchpeople turn out to be our best teachers. They teach us how they want to be loved and cared for. I don't want to take anything away from the capable mentors I have had along the way, and I have had some good ones, but churchpeople are the ones who do the real work.

One of my seminary classmates disagrees with me about this. She spent much of her career as a kind of bishop, though Baptists would never call them that. And in her work she says that she had to do lots of teaching about how church members should get along, how they should treat their pastors and each other. I don't doubt that that's true, that sometimes churches need help in order to become healthy, but I still think that, in a relationship, it helps when the other person says, "Yes, that, please, but not that other thing you do."

I forget now how far along I was in my career before I realized that my people knew me pretty well. They had seen me on my good days, but they had also seen me on my bad ones. Over time they knew how I would respond to most situations. And the thing is that they were, by and large, all things considered, with only one or two exceptions, a forgiving bunch. They tolerated a lot of mistakes along the way because they sometimes saw in me what I could not see in myself. My best teachers in life have always been like that.

Once, at the church I served in Wheaton, I made what I thought was a small change to the order of worship on Christmas Eve, my first at the church, not knowing that there are *never* small changes to Christmas Eve worship. When I looked over the bulletin from the previous year, I saw what I thought was an odd way of singing "Silent Night" at the end of worship. The choir would sing "Silent Night," while the congregation would sing a partner tune known as "Peace, Peace," something I had never heard before. And since I had never heard it before, I was pretty sure that I didn't like it and that we could do better. So, out went "Peace, Peace."

What I didn't know, but what I could easily have found out, if I had asked one random person in the congregation, was that the church had sung this odd song every year on Christmas Eve for as long as anyone could remember. People came to the 11:00 service on Christmas Eve not so that they could hear the new preacher's clever insights into the second chapter of Luke, but so that they could sing one of their favorite songs while holding lit candles in a darkened sanctuary.

Of course, I heard about it almost immediately. Instead of a cheery "Merry Christmas" at the church door after worship, what I heard from nearly everyone that night was a not-very-friendly "What happened to 'Peace, Peace'?" For a few terrible days I thought that might be my last Christmas at the Wheaton church. But—here's the truly astonishing part of the story—they forgave me. Not right away, but more quickly than I expected. They forgave me and decided to give me a closer look. Today, in fact, I seem to be the only one who remembers the incident. That's forgiveness.

A seminary president once told me that pastors aren't fired anymore for doctrinal errors; they're fired, he said, for making "dumbass mistakes." Make enough dumbass mistakes—or one big one—and out you go. It's a miracle that more of us aren't shown the door in our first months of ministry with a new congregation. But churchpeople practice forgiveness most of the time, and in their forgiveness they teach pastors how to be pastors, how to act like servant leaders instead of the church know-it-all.

This experience of forgiveness from congregation after congregation produced in me a kind of humility I didn't learn at seminary. And then, once humbled, I began to learn all kinds of things about being a pastor.

MOST PEOPLE ARE SURPRISED to learn that I did not want to be a pastor when I was growing up, assuming that all pastors know from an early age what they are going to do with their lives. Pastors like that may exist, but I was not one of them.

What I wanted more than anything, as I mentioned, was to play baseball for the Detroit Tigers, but this turned out to be one prayer among many God chose not to answer, at least not in the way I hoped. When my athletic career died a painful death in high school, it wasn't clear to me what I would become or what exactly I should pray for. I stopped praying about a career, and for a long time I stopped praying altogether.

What was always clear to me was how much my parents and grandparents, especially my mother, wanted me to become a pastor. Whenever my mother talked about her father, who died a year before I was born, and who always seemed to be facing the loss of a job or health or something, she always added, as a critical element to the story, that he had always wanted to be a pastor and that he would have been "so proud" to see me become one. She must have thought that, in the constant retelling, this story would one day, at long last, get my attention. This story, however, always had the opposite of the desired effect.

Vocation is not something that can be wished on anyone. I have always thought that vocation, our calling in life, should come from outside of ourselves, a voice that speaks to us clearly and unmistakably.

But even now I struggle to say what that means. It sounds like something I might have learned in Sunday school, which is where I learned most of the important things about my faith, and it's how the Bible speaks about call. What seems clear is that God called all sorts of people—first by getting their attention, which wasn't always easy, and then by telling them what to do. To a young Jeremiah, God is supposed to have said, "I appointed you a prophet to the nations." Jeremiah grasps enough of what this might mean, because in the next breath he says, "Ah, Lord God—I am only a boy." He didn't like the prospect of being a "prophet to the nations." He could feel the weight of what he was being called to do.

Parker Palmer has written helpfully to those thinking about vocation. In his book *Let Your Life Speak: Listening for the Voice of Vocation*, he encourages readers to pay attention to what their lives are saying as a way of discerning their calling in life. "Listen to your life," he says.

I see the wisdom in that advice. I have even offered it to others. Paying attention to one's gifts and life experiences is undoubtedly a step in "discerning one's call" (as pastors like to put it) or in "figuring out what to do with your life" (as most other people put it). I would not have found my way to seminary, and then to parish ministry, if I had not done a careful assessment of my gifts and interests, if I hadn't listened, as Palmer likes to say, to my life.

But something about this "listen to your life" advice has always troubled me too. It's not that God doesn't speak in this way, but I have always preferred burning bushes to still, small voices. I'm one of those people who needs a trumpet fanfare to get my attention. God used a small earthquake to get Isaiah to pay attention, and now I know why. Frankly, I wanted to know that what I was doing with my life was more than fulfilling my own dreams and ambitions, like playing professional baseball. And to me that implies something or someone beyond myself—in other words, that there is One Who Calls.

When God calls people in the Bible, particularly in the Old Testament, they're often surprised, and not in a good way, like Jeremiah. The impression is that being called by God is the last thing on their minds at that particular moment. Often they resist. Sometimes they're terrified. And they almost always complain that they're not up to the task. They see, almost immediately, that God's call will take them in an entirely different direction with their lives than the one they had in mind for themselves.

Beyond that, God always seems to call the least likely people. Moses was a murderer on the run. David was the youngest of eight sons and a shepherd, not a highly regarded way of life, then or now. And Mary was a young peasant girl from Nazareth. Yet God saw in each of them what no one else could see. And when they didn't have what was required, God supplied what they needed.

William Willimon, in his memoir *Accidental Preacher*, points to Jesus's disciples as further examples of "least likely" people to be called. Willimon refers to them bluntly as "remarkably mediocre, untalented, lackluster yokels" and writes that they had neither the innate talent nor the inner yearning to do God's work. And yet, Jesus called them, one by one, to follow along.

I have always been a little troubled by how quickly and willingly the disciples responded to Jesus's call. A few of them—Peter and Andrew, James and John—seemed to me a little too eager to leave their nets behind. I wondered why I was not more like them, eager to follow God's plan for my life.

On a pilgrimage to Israel with a group of church members, I remember a boat ride on the Sea of Galilee, a brief cruise most tour groups are expected to take, and I noticed four young Israeli men at the back of the boat. They had helped us board at the start of the voyage, and they would help us off at the end. But in between they seemed to have little to do but smoke cigarettes and watch a bunch of Americans who were smitten with the idea of sailing around the Sea of Galilee where, just imagine, Jesus himself had once sailed.

The four young men were either in their late teens or early twenties, and I suddenly made what I thought was a preacher's clever observation. Those young men at the back of the boat were Peter and Andrew, James and John. I never learned their real names, but I became convinced that's who they were. Bored, cynical (about the piety of most American Christians), restless, and ready to say yes to just about anything that would get them out of this boat, away from these Americans, and into something more interesting.

As I imagine it, Peter and Andrew and James and John looked at Jesus, and then they looked back at Zebedee mending the nets along with all the other old men, and they realized in a heartbeat that they didn't want to spend their entire lives doing that.

Jesus, get me out of here. Follow you? Okay.

I resisted my call to ministry at first, and then, later on, I embraced it. It was, I thought, the path to a more exciting life, with growing churches and surging endowments and lots of social esteem. Then, like Jesus's disciples, I sometimes wondered where this call would take me. In Mark 10, James and John reportedly said to Jesus: "Grant us to sit, one at your right hand and one at your left, in your glory." A preferred seat in the kingdom of God? A place of honor? That's what I wanted too. A good salary and a housing allowance, four weeks of vacation and two more weeks for something called "study leave." Medical insurance and pension. I never said it aloud, but I know it was there. I wanted an important seat in the kingdom of God too.

And Jesus said to them, "You do not know what you are asking."

I Was Paid Well, After All

Tell your stories. If people wanted you to write warmly about them, they should have behaved better.

Anne Lamott, *Bird by Bird:*
Some Instructions on Writing and Life

Some pastors have framed diplomas, awards, and certificates of appreciation hanging around their walls, bearing witness to proud accomplishments. I had a sewer permit, an irritating reminder of construction setbacks and personal inadequacy.

Heidi B. Neumark, *Breathing Space:*
A Spiritual Journey in the South Bronx

I REMEMBER WAKING UP ONE MORNING in Zürich, Switzerland, where I served my last congregation before retiring, and I remember waking up mad. I was mad about something that had happened years before moving to Zürich. I'm no longer certain why, but on this particular morning I remembered something so painful that it had me clenching my teeth before I opened my eyes.

Maybe I was at a good place in my life just then and could finally allow myself to remember what had happened, to process the feeling at last and maybe, God willing, to move beyond it.

The memory, though it was more than that, was of a certain colleague, a member of a previous church staff. As I think about it now, and as I thought about it that morning in Zürich, I realize that I should have seen it coming. When I first met the person, I had the uneasy feeling that it would not go well between us, that our working relationship would not be smooth, that there would be trouble, sooner rather than later. Also, if I saw it coming, then that means I'm partly to blame, doesn't it? I must have allowed it to happen. Or at least I did nothing to prevent it. So, I remember being angry with myself too.

What I did wrong, which seems so clear in hindsight, was to trust someone I should never have trusted, not in a million years. But I did. I acted in good faith. I prayed with this person. I shared a hymnbook as we sang together and worshiped. I sometimes had a queasy feeling as I did all of that, but I trusted anyway, because that's what you do on a church staff. You put yourself out there; you become vulnerable. One time this person even said to me, "Doug, I want to know what's in your heart." But I wasn't sure I wanted to say what was in my heart. I was certain that this person didn't care all that much what was in my heart.

Betrayal is what happens when you act in good faith, become vulnerable, extend yourself for someone else, and then that person turns out not to be trustworthy after all, not to have your best interests in mind, not to care at all about you. What is it about betrayal that hurts so much? The coldness of it? The calculation? No, it's how casual and unthinking it can be. Hannah Arendt once wrote that "the sad truth is that most evil is done by people who never make up their minds to be good or evil." I think that's true. What hurts so much is just this—it wasn't calculated.

Remembering and then reliving the experience during those pre-dawn hours in Zürich was what I needed to do. I needed to unclench and let go, which I couldn't do until I acknowledged to myself the sheer awfulness of what had happened, the extent to which I had been betrayed, and all the sorry details of it. I couldn't move on, much less forgive, until I had remembered every bit of it.

It's not the first time something like this has happened to me, being betrayed by a colleague. You don't get to my age without having been betrayed once or twice along the way. Life is like that. I remember another incident, from a long time ago, that felt like a kick to the gut. I felt at the time as though the wind had been knocked out of me. I picked up a phone to call a lawyer. I was sure I had a case. I would sue. That, I thought, would make things right.

But Fred Anderson, who was my senior pastor all those years ago in Harrisburg, someone who knows me well, listened to me tell the story and said, "Doug, let it go." And I did. I don't remember anymore how I did it. It happened rather quickly. I put down the phone. I deleted the angry letter I had written. I started to breathe again. It was over. I hadn't thought about it in years—not until this other betrayal, as a matter of fact. And then, surprisingly, there it was again.

Betrayal and grief have much in common. Every loss, like every betrayal, reminds us of every other loss we have ever experienced and how bad they feel. Every betrayal is a reason not to trust anymore, not to be vulnerable, not to put yourself out there.

I SHOULD MENTION that I have had mostly good relationships in the church and with my colleagues, which is one reason, I suppose, that the few difficult relationships have been so painful. By far the majority of those I have known and worked with over the years have been dedicated, hardworking, skilled, and lovely people. I have learned a great deal about ministry by working alongside them. I became a better pastor because of their example. I covered their responsibilities when they needed someone to take over for them, because I always knew they would do the same for me. I can honestly say that these relationships kept me going in moments when I was ready to throw in the towel. I loved them, and I knew they loved me.

But the exceptions to the rule have been painful.

I'm not sure what it is, but church staffs are unlike most other work environments. I'm not a veteran, but I suspect that there are similarities between a church staff and a group of soldiers. For one thing, you believe in what you're doing, the mission, at a level most other businesses and organizations can't begin to match. You have to trust the person next to you. You must put your life in their hands. That may sound like a strong statement, but after forty years of working in the trenches I think it's true. All of my jobs before working in the church were just that—jobs. I worked the required number of hours, and I then took home my pay. Sometimes the work was interesting; sometimes it wasn't. But I always knew that those other things I did were jobs.

Churchwork was (and is) different, and I knew that was true from the first day. I knew that I was involved in something far larger than myself. And so I committed myself to it; I threw myself into it. I'm not sure I was ready to die for it, as a soldier presumably would be, but I would work hard enough for the church that my health sometimes suffered. I would work hard enough that I sometimes neglected my marriage and my family. There was a time, which my wife will never forget, when I left her the day of her mother's funeral to drive back home, so that I could lead worship the next day. I said goodbye at the reception following the service, got in the car, and drove three hours to do something that my colleagues could have done for me, if only I had asked. Church members would have understood too. I told myself that going home, toughing it out, and preaching when I didn't feel like it, was what dedicated pastors did.

ONE OF THE BEST STAFFS I was ever a part of was my first one. I was an associate pastor, and there were a couple of pastoral interns, a Christian education director, a social worker, a musician, a church administrator, and a few others. It's hard to put my finger on what made the experience so good, but much of it undoubtedly was the senior pastor—the vision and passion he brought to the work. He worked harder than any of us, was there earlier, and stayed later. Not only that, but he had time for each one of us. I remember that our staff meetings, where we studied the biblical text for the following Sunday, often felt like doctoral seminars. We pushed each other to learn and grow and be the best at whatever our job descriptions required. There was also, as I mentioned, the Brown Shoe Award. We cared deeply for each other.

One of the first lessons in staff relationships I learned from Fred was that I could say anything to him in his office. If I had an issue with him, if I needed to get something off my chest, I was to go in and close the door and say what was on my mind. But outside his door, in the company of church members, Fred expected that we would be singing from the same hymnbook. I took him up on the invitation, too, more than once. I called and asked if he had "a minute," and then I would walk over to his office, close the door behind me, and complain loudly about something I didn't understand or something he had said. What was good about those moments was that Fred always listened, patiently, and there were never consequences for disagreeing.

For years afterward, when I would come upon a thorny issue in the church, I would ask myself, "What would Fred do in this situation?" I admired him and have told him so. Beyond that, I knew that he respected my gifts, which were still clearly in the developmental phase. He found ways for me to succeed and then allowed me to receive all the credit.

I was still finding my way as preacher, and so Fred would pick me up early on those rare Sunday mornings when I was scheduled to preach, and after making coffee he would sit at the back of an empty church, at the sound and light console, while I awkwardly preached my sermon. Most of the time, when I was finished, he would say, "Do it again." And I did. He flattered me by telling me that I had content worth listening to; what I needed, he said, was a delivery as good as my words. He invested his time in me, and I responded by wanting to be worthy of his investment.

Some of my seminary classmates were not so lucky. Their first experiences of the church were plainly negative. I know, because we would get together those first years and talk about them over pitchers of beer. No one in my circle of friends dropped out of ministry altogether, but a couple of years after ordination two of them had already moved in a different direction, away from serving a congregation. One went to work for the denomination in an administrative position, and another returned to school for a further degree and an academic career. The rest of us carried on the best we could in our congregations.

The career trajectory that was laid out for me and other MDiv students by faculty and administrators at Princeton was to get a position as an associate pastor in a large church immediately after graduation. The idea was to learn from a skilled senior pastor for a few years, then work in a medium-sized church to gain administrative experience, and finally become the senior pastor of progressively larger churches. I should mention that the second half of this career plan—becoming the pastor of a large church—was available, almost exclusively, to male students. Lots of my classmates, women and men, found associate pastor positions after graduation, but few if any of the women were able to take the next step. And because there were few large churches, not many male classmates were going to complete this career trajectory either.

The ultimate destination, which only one of us was going to reach, was Fifth Avenue Presbyterian Church in New York City, at one time the largest Presbyterian church in the city. Bryant Kirkland was the senior pastor there when I was a Princeton student, and on Mondays he would teach preaching classes at the seminary. These were not so much occasions to learn about preaching (I remember little of what he said), but to admire someone who had made it, who had blazed the path that we were expected to follow.

Kirkland was polished in a way that most of us were not, that most of us would never be. His suits were expensive. His silvery hair was trimmed just so. He even had a noticeable tan, which I found puzzling in February. The unspoken message was that we were to be like him. Somehow, he found time to read books (lots of them), to write thoughtful, literate sermons, and to administer a church with several thousand members. His sermon titles were provocative enough, we were told, to get people off the Fifth Avenue bus and into the sanctuary. Accepting a call to become an associate pastor of a large downtown church in Harrisburg, Pennsylvania, was my first step on this path. I continued to read books (as many as I could), but my hair, tan, and wardrobe still needed considerable work.

I ALSO WORKED ON STAFFS that were not as good as my first one. Sometimes the problem was one person who didn't fit, who would have been happier somewhere else, who needed to start looking for a new position. Another time I thought the whole staff culture was unhealthy. My memory of that particular church is one of constant turnover. I replaced nearly everyone on the staff over a five-year period, and still the feeling seemed off, not what I thought it should be. I had my theories about what was causing it, but I never did manage to sort it out. I lost lots of sleep thinking about it, and by the end of my tenure at that church I was exhausted.

Early in my ministry a new staff member was not being well received by church members. She came to us with excellent credentials and strong recommendations from her faculty. I thought she was fun to be with and as dedicated as anyone I had ever known. But for some reason the fit wasn't right, and I grew weary of phone calls from unhappy church members. Finally, I brought in the Lombard Mennonite Peace Center, an organization in our area that mediated church conflict. Our entire church was not in conflict, but one of its important ministries was. It needed attention, and I remember not knowing what else to do. The mediator was helpful. Problems were identified. Unhealthy expectations were addressed openly and honestly. But the entire process, several thousand dollars later, ended in a resignation and hurt feelings. I can feel them now.

Over the years I have had colleagues who embezzled from the church, told obvious lies at staff meetings about their work, took a week of vacation without telling anyone and without leaving contact information, brought trauma from childhood sexual abuse into relationships with male coworkers, had sex with church members in the apartment owned by the church, lied about credentials to get the job, dated a member of the church board (two separate occasions), organized and advertised a conference on a controversial topic without receiving approval in advance from me or the church board, loudly berated another staff member during coffee hour in front of church members, and more. One colleague who, I learned later, was having problems in his marriage slept in his office for a month before acknowledging that there was "something going on" in his personal life. These examples are only the first ones I thought of. There are more.

It's something of a cliché to blame one's seminary training for problems in the parish. "I never had a course at seminary about this" is a common refrain among pastors. In churchwork I have had to become an expert (or at least somewhat proficient) at repairing boilers and roofs and organ pipes, applying for building permits, hiring architects, striping a parking lot, responding to a termite infestation, raising millions of dollars for a building campaign, and getting law enforcement cooperation for particularly large funerals. These subjects weren't covered during my seminary training, and to be honest there is no way to prepare for everything a pastor encounters in church life. So, like all of my classmates, I learned on the job.

One of the most helpful, supportive groups of people I have ever worked with was the personnel committee. I don't know what I would have done without them. In the Presbyterian churches I served, personnel committees were typically made up of business owners, corporate executives, lawyers, and (one time) a school district superintendent. (An early mentor warned me against inviting "schoolteachers" to join the personnel committee because, as he put it, with a wink, "They don't make enough money. Always find people for the personnel committee who make a lot more than you do.") I learned a great deal from these people, I trusted their judgment, and from time to time I disagreed with them. When a colleague embezzled money, for example, their inclination was to go to the state's attorney and press charges. I argued against that approach, for reasons I no longer remember, and then later regretted not following their advice. I would not have survived for long had it not been for the personnel committees I have known over the years.

And yet, looking back, I wonder about all of this. I understand that larger congregations are more complex and therefore require more sophisticated management tools and personnel policies. As systems grow, they require more careful thought and attention. My happiest days of ministry were those when a capable administrator handled the day-to-day management of buildings and staff and computers. I was happy to let all of it go, so that I could focus on—but that's just it, isn't it? What is it that a pastor is supposed to be doing? I could get rid of tasks that I didn't like, but even now I couldn't say exactly what I should have been doing instead. Not encouraging the staff and spending time with them? Not being concerned about the building and making sure that it was preserved and maintained? How is it possible to be the pastor, the leader of the flock, and not do these things and more?

Large churches, like the ones I served for much of my career, have been popular because they can offer so much more, a smorgasbord of activities and ministries, all administered by talented and well-trained staff. And smaller churches, in contrast, have often struggled because they couldn't keep up. American Christians bring their consumer instincts to church, and they expect—and typically demand—that all of their needs will be met. If those needs aren't met, there is always another, often larger, church down the street.

I shouldn't complain about my large church experience. I was paid well, after all, and I enjoyed all the benefits that go with wealth and prestige and power. Not long ago I was able to retire comfortably because I worked in churches that could afford to pay me well. But something about all of this strikes me as wrong. I find myself thinking about the churches I served as falling short of what they could and should have been—places of grace and mercy and hope, places where struggling people could find a home and acceptance and new life.

I wish I had put less of my time into management and more into living out the gospel, which was what interested me about ministry in the first place.

10

We Welcome You

If your understanding of the divine made you kinder, more empathetic, and impelled you to express sympathy in concrete acts of loving-kindness, this was good theology. But if your notion of God made you unkind, belligerent, cruel, or self-righteous, or if it led you to kill in God's name, it was bad theology.

Karen Armstrong, *The Spiral Staircase:*
My Climb Out of Darkness

One of the great challenges of contemporary pastoral ministry is having something more important to do in our ministry than simply offering love and service to our people.

William H. Willimon, *Pastor: The Theology*
and Practice of Ordained Ministry

My longest—and in many ways happiest—church experience was in Wheaton, Illinois, where I served as senior pastor for thirteen years and raised my two daughters to adulthood. I had interviewed with a few other churches before accepting the call to Wheaton, but the church in Wheaton seemed like the best fit, though even now I couldn't say exactly why.

At a church in North Carolina, where I had also interviewed, the search committee took me on a tour of the church buildings and sanctuary. When we were in the sanctuary, they told me—a few of them with glistening eyes—about how their former pastor, now retired, had always arranged the flowers "just so" before worship. He took "such care" with everything. And Sunday mornings were always "so beautiful."

I like flowers too, but this was not the message I wanted to hear. The church in Wheaton, on the other hand, had been through "a difficult season of ministry," the euphemism that pastors and church members use to refer to the time they nearly gave up and quit. Without giving all of the particulars, that season for the Wheaton church had been undeniably difficult. The membership had declined by hundreds of members. Giving was down. And the look of defeat was obvious on the faces of the search committee members. At one point during a daylong interview, I asked them if they were as gloomy about the church's future as they sounded.

I like the climate better in North Carolina, but the church in Illinois was a challenge I couldn't turn down. My wife and I decided that we would accept the call and give it our best shot. The odds were not in our favor, but if things didn't work out, if my tenure at the church was short, as we half-expected, we decided that this would be my last church. I would quit ministry and do something else with my life. We even bought a house that had one important quality we liked—namely, quick resale potential. It was in a neighborhood with hundreds of other houses that looked pretty much the same—same floor plan, same inexpensive construction. There were street names such as Buckingham, Cornwell, Somerset, and Canterbury, suggesting houses that were more upscale than they actually were.

Surprisingly, though, some of the best years of my life were spent at our house at 1908 Somerset Lane, in my not-very-upscale house, with my wife and young daughters.

I was thirty-eight when I moved with my family to Wheaton, and I had all the characteristics that a church like the one in Wheaton was looking for at the time: I was a young, white, and heterosexual male. As a bonus, I was married and had an attractive family. My wife and daughters seemed as though they would actively support me and the church's ministry, and importantly they might attract other young families to the church. I had a brand-new DMin degree from Princeton Theological Seminary, and it was important to them, as it is to many mainline congregations, to call their pastor "Doctor Somebody." As a bonus, I was originally from the Midwest and looked as though I had the modesty, sobriety, and lack of spontaneity that many people associate with that part of the country.

"IF THINGS DON'T WORK OUT in Wheaton, I'll quit and do something else" turned out to be a good attitude to have about my work. In hindsight, going for broke might have been a better strategy at other churches I served. I woke up most days and thought, "Things can't get much worse around here, so why not give my latest harebrained idea a shot?"

Early in my years at the Wheaton church, I noticed a hallway near the kitchen with portraits of former pastors. Lots of churches have a similar rogues' gallery, and I have disliked every one I've seen. So, when I received a call one day, a year or so into my tenure, from the photographer who had made two or three of the most recent portraits, I said, "Thank you, but we won't be doing that."

The church, I believed then, as I do now, is not about the pastor. I am naïve in this belief, of course. The church is usually very much about the pastor. But, over the years, that's a stance I've taken, one I continue to be proud of. "What we do here is not going to be about me," I said to members when they heard about the rough treatment I had given to the photographer. "If we put up any portraits, we'll put up portraits of the members, not me." I'm surprised now that I spoke so forcefully. Church members seemed to like it too. Or else they were willing to go along with it, because, as I mentioned, they were desperate. I soon realized, in fact, that they were determined to keep me around and make the relationship work. They eventually accepted most of the ideas, harebrained or not, that I came up with.

Histories of local churches, often written by longtime members and former high school English teachers, are typically not very good reading. (Sorry, but that's true.) And one of the reasons is that they are typically arranged as a timeline of former pastors, so that church members end up telling their stories as a series of eras: "Then, after Dr. Stavrakos, Dr. Brouwer became our pastor." I know that this is how history usually works out in practice, but I was determined during my first years in Wheaton either to rewrite history or to prove history wrong. I knew that I was young and brash, but I was determined that the church in Wheaton was going to be different. We were going to break out of the mold and not be "church as usual." And, to a surprising degree, we were not "church as usual," but I think now that we should have broken the mold entirely. I should have been more brash, not less. We had our chances, but too often we didn't take them.

PRIOR TO MY ARRIVAL, the church was known in the community for marching in the US flag at the beginning of worship. Young people from the congregation would proudly walk both a US flag and a

Christian flag down the center aisle, place the flags in brass stands, and then take their seats up front with the pastors, waiting throughout the service to take the flags out again at the end.

I had never seen this before, even though I was familiar with the rituals of formal Presbyterian worship. I didn't know what to make of it, but I knew that this situation would need some careful and deliberate thought. After no more than a second of careful and deliberate thought, I moved the flags out of the sanctuary and into the fellowship hall, hoping no one would notice. Bruce Walker, a retired US Navy commander, who during his career specialized in naval intelligence, noticed right away and without any hesitation moved the flags back into the sanctuary.

He found me after worship that Sunday and said, apologetically, "I know the flags are starting to look bad. I'll get new ones this week and polish up the brass flag stands." He thought I was embarrassed by how worn and shabby they looked.

Bruce and I came to know each other well over the thirteen years that I was his pastor, but this first interaction set the tone for our relationship. I decided not to back down. I told Bruce that flags didn't belong in the sanctuary, except maybe on special occasions. The focus of worship, I argued, should always be on God. He seemed dubious about this, but to his credit he kept listening to me. I suggested, as a compromise, that we march the flags in only on special occasions like Memorial Day weekend. Remarkably, Bruce agreed. But then, unexpectedly, he found several other, flag-worthy holidays that I knew nothing about. Still, the issue was resolved to Bruce's satisfaction, and the church got new flags and shined-up brass flag stands. And, along the way, I received an education in flag etiquette, learning among other things that the flag always belongs on the pulpit side of the sanctuary, so that it is visible over the preacher's shoulder.

This compromise over flags, however, was not the end of the story with Bruce. He told me early in my tenure that the church had a mission opportunity with the Great Lakes Naval Training Center, also located in a Chicago suburb. His proposal was to send a bus to the training center on Thanksgiving morning and bring back as many scared recruits to the church as would fit in the bus. Then, the recruits, two by two, would be assigned to families within the congregation who would "stuff" (Bruce's word) the recruits with Thanksgiving dinner, allow them to make phone calls to families back home, and get them back to the church by late afternoon for the return ride to the base. I liked the idea.

For the initial announcement to the congregation, Bruce wore his dress uniform to the lectern and joked that it had shrunk in the closet, a joke he would repeat every year for the next ten years, whenever he made the Thanksgiving announcement. As it turned out, more recruits signed up that first year than we expected, and so the following year we sent two buses to the base.

The tradition grew from there, so that one year when the recruits arrived and sat in the sanctuary for my words of welcome, I remember that the church was completely filled with naval recruits, all sitting stiffly, shoulder to shoulder, as if at attention. Each year I would welcome them, offer a prayer of thanks for their service (which hadn't technically begun), lead in the singing of the Navy Hymn ("Eternal Father, Strong to Save"), and then assign the recruits to members of the church. I'm still not sure why, but the annual Thanksgiving dinner with naval recruits turned out to be one of the most gratifying things we did together as a church, a ministry opportunity that uniquely fit our culture. All thanks to Commander Bruce Walker.

AND NOW AN EXAMPLE of an opportunity squandered.

During my years in Wheaton, the church enjoyed considerable growth. Hundreds of new members joined in a relatively short period of time. At one point, by my estimate, more than half of the membership had become members during my tenure. To accommodate the growth, the church decided to undertake a building campaign. As the architects put it, using a new language I was learning to speak, we would "double the church's footprint." The church is located on a single city block, and at the time it consisted of a sanctuary, a parish house, a parsonage (or manse), and a Christian education building. But no parking lot. The city block was mostly a lovely lawn, which was what motorists noticed when they drove past on busy Ellis Avenue.

The parsonage, which housed a pastoral counseling center, was torn down to make way for an expanded classroom building and gymnasium. A parking lot was added next to the church, and as a result the lawn shrank considerably. There was also a new front entrance to the church. The architects said it "looked like arms opening to the community," which I liked.

Inside the new entrance, an atrium with sky lights, a mural was commissioned and hung, and the words on the mural were "We welcome you, as we would welcome Christ himself." It was my paraphrase of words that St. Francis once used: "When a stranger arrives, Christ is present."

All of that was so much fun! And then someone said, "You know, a church always changes after a building campaign. It takes on a new identity. What is our new identity going to be?" I panicked. I realized at that moment that we had done something big, far bigger than I realized, but we hadn't thought through all of the implications. What was this church going to be? I had in mind, of course, that the church would be welcoming, but how welcoming? We were bursting at the seams with relatively affluent white people. Also, straight people and traditional family units. But what about other people? What about single people, for example? Gay and lesbian people? People of color? Would they be welcome too? How wide were we going to fling open our doors?

For a while we discussed a name change. The name First Presbyterian Church of Wheaton, to my mind, didn't suggest welcome so much as wealth, power, and prestige, which we had in abundance. What if, I wondered, the church really embraced the direction in which we seemed to be moving? What if we became a church with arms wide open to our community? And what if we changed our name to reflect that spirit? Church of the Open Arms and Open Hearts?

Okay, not that, but something that communicated the sentiment.

I made an appointment with Bob Reynolds, the executive presbyter of Chicago Presbytery, and over lunch told him that we were considering a name change. I said, "We probably can't just do that, which is why I'm having lunch with you." He seemed annoyed with me, which would not have been the first time, and he said, "Doug, when have we ever said no to you?" And with that, of course, the challenge was thrown back to me. He seemed to say that we could do it if we wanted—a few committee approvals, maybe, but nothing too difficult. The point was, the presbytery was not going to stand in our way.

So, what would we call ourselves? What name would suggest a welcome to all?

And then the moment was lost. The brashness I had embraced at the beginning had already begun to fade, and with it an opportunity to do something significant disappeared. Church life became busier than before because of the new building. Additional programming was added because of the new gym. And so, swept along by the strong current of day-to-day ministry and continued growth, we missed an opportunity to break the mold of "church as usual," to be what the church *should* be, instead of what it occasionally aspires to be.

The opportunity lost was not only the name change, but also the congregation-wide rethinking of what welcome really means.

MORE REMARKABLE THAN THE BUILDING CAMPAIGN, the story that remains most gratifying to me is the number of people from the Wheaton church who responded to a call to ministry during these years. Nine women and men, mostly young, but three at midlife, made a decision to go to seminary. Eight of the nine continued to ordination; the other, a physician, decided to pursue her ministry through medicine. Three are now retired, leaving six still serving churches in the Presbyterian Church (USA.)

The nine include (in alphabetical order) Sarah Brouwer (my daughter), Andrew Gifford, Peter Henry, PhD, Mabel Koshy, MD, Andrew Kukla, Patricia Locke, Sarah Iliff McGill, Ericka Parkinson-Kilbourne, and Diane Slocum.

NOT EVERYONE, AS IT TURNS OUT, is enthusiastic about a growing church. I wish I had a dollar for every complaint I listened to about the lack of parking. But finding a place to park is just the beginning of the problem of a growing church.

As often as churches say they want to grow, the truth is that growth can be difficult and painful. Growth changes what had been safe and comfortable and familiar. Growth brings new people, and with them new ideas and new ways of thinking. And as I mentioned, growth became important enough to me that I forgot the "go for broke" attitude I started with.

At the Wheaton church, new member classes were held each month. I had learned at a church growth seminar that asking new members to attend a series of new member classes, never less than four, was the way to communicate an important message. And the important message we wanted to communicate, according to the seminar speakers, was high commitment, high participation, and high engagement. People should know, they said, that we were going to demand something from them. Low-commitment churches were dying, we were told, while high-commitment churches, counterintuitively, were growing. I accepted this conclusion without ever seeing the data.

One of the seminar speakers, Donn Moomaw, a former All-American football player at UCLA, told of a time that Ronald and Nancy Reagan asked to join his Presbyterian church in Bel Air, California. The pastor told the former president and his wife that four classes were required—on four consecutive Sunday evenings—a commitment he knew they would be unable to make until the Reagan presidency was over. But Moomaw held firm, and he said to those attending the seminar, "If I can say no to the President of the United States, then you can say no to the people who say they want to join your church, but who can't make a commitment." And then, with a satisfied smile, Moomaw told us Ronald and Nancy Reagan joined the Bel Air church following the Reagan presidency.

I confess that I was suitably impressed with this story and brought the moral of the story to the church in Wheaton. We held firm with our requirement concerning membership classes, not that many people were resisting, and we continued to grow. One Sunday, seventy-seven new members stood at the front of the sanctuary, and the welcoming ritual took several minutes as we read each of their names. It was quite a morning, one I will never forget. I was so happy that I wanted to do cartwheels across the front of the church, but when I looked into the congregation, I saw some longtime members with tears in their eyes. They weren't happy at all, and they were not about to do cartwheels. Their church, as they explained it to me later, was changing. They used to know everyone, and now they would look around on Sunday mornings and see only a few familiar faces. They didn't know, they told me, if they belonged anymore.

I MET MANY WONDERFUL PEOPLE IN WHEATON, I grew close to them and loved them deeply, I enjoyed my work most of the time, and I feel gratitude today for being given the opportunity. My daughters look back on the church of their childhood not uncritically, but with a fair amount of fondness. One of them, changed enough by the experience, became a Presbyterian pastor. The other daughter reports having a hard time finding a church in adulthood where she feels as welcome and as loved as she did at the Wheaton church.

On the Sunday afternoon after my farewell, I sat exhausted on my outdoor patio and read all of the notes and cards, hundreds of them, that the church had collected for me. I was overwhelmed. I cried more that day than I did before or have since.

But even an experience as good as the one I had in Wheaton raises questions. It was, probably, an opportunity squandered—a "go for broke" attitude that gave way, as many churches do, to complacency. I wonder about the building we built and the money we spent. I wonder about the historic parsonage we tore down to make way for the new building. I wonder about the parking lot, which, to be honest, seemed to benefit the choir more than anyone, because they were the first to arrive on Sunday mornings. And I wonder about all those new member classes and how we could have used the time in a better way.

History, if history has an opinion about large suburban churches, may not render a kind judgment on everything we did.

Dollar for Dollar

The church is not meant to call men and women out of the world into a safe religious enclave but to call them out in order to send them back as agents of God's kingship.

Lesslie Newbigin, *Foolishness to the Greeks*

We would like a church that again asserts that God, not nations, rules the world, that the boundaries of God's kingdom transcend those of Caesar, and that the main political task of the church is the formation of people who see clearly the cost of discipleship and are willing to pay the price.

Stanley Hauerwas and William H. Willimon,
Resident Aliens: Life in the Christian Colony

MANY OF MY SEMINARY CLASSMATES liked to say that they embraced a therapeutic model of ministry. They wanted to become pastoral counselors, therapists, and chaplains, and they were clear about this from the first day of classes.

This made no sense to me, but the reason, I learned, was simple: church staff positions, except as Christian educators, would not be open to them. Even in denominations where women were ordained, the number of openings for women would be small. There was no hope for any woman of becoming pastor of the Fifth Avenue Presbyterian Church in New York City. Not in the twentieth century.

I had no interest in becoming a chaplain, and I was dismissive of the therapeutic model in my conversations with classmates. I would have said at the time that the gospel compels us to look beyond ourselves. I would have argued that the therapeutic model was inward-looking and self-absorbed. And I would have been right about that, but I was mostly blind to the seriousness of the situation, the lack of other choices. As a white, heterosexual male, I could do pretty much whatever I wanted after graduation, while many of my classmates could not. The people sitting next to me in class felt a call to ministry that was no less profound than mine; they were simply being realistic about what they would be allowed to do.

As it turned out, for all of my early protests about it, the pastoral (or therapeutic) dimension of my work has always been a thoroughly enjoyable part of my ministry. To put it simply, I loved the work of being a pastor. I loved the hospital calls and the home visits. I loved seeing people in my office when they called and said they needed to talk. One of my preaching professors said that pastors earned the right to be prophetic in the pulpit when they do pastoral work during the week, by which he meant visiting the sick and making calls on the homebound and being available when people were hurting. But I was seldom prophetic in my preaching, even when I had earned the right to be. I seldom exercised that right.

I could see injustice in the world as clearly as anyone. I didn't experience it firsthand, of course, not in mostly white, southeast Grand Rapids, where I grew up, but I came of age in the late 1960s. Even from the comfortable suburban neighborhood where I was raised, I knew that many people around the world, and many in my own country, were in desperate need. Moreover, when I became a pastor, I knew that church members needed to look beyond their own needs. Not that the needs (and complaints) of church members were unimportant; it's that in looking beyond themselves, I thought, they would see that their needs (and complaints) were comparatively small and insignificant.

And then of course—how could we forget—there was also the gospel mandate to feed the hungry, offer drink to the thirsty, clothe the naked, visit the sick, and so on.

I was first introduced to the Confession of 1967 when I became a Presbyterian. The Confession of 1967 came to be written in response to the racial turmoil of the 1950s and 1960s, and then through its emphasis on reconciliation became particularly useful to the church during the cultural revolution of the late 1960s. The Confession of 1967 describes the church as a living organism, inhaling and exhaling, and even though I had spent my entire life in the church, I had never heard such vivid language to describe what the church was called to be: "The church *gathers* to praise God," the Confession declares, and "it *disperses* to serve God . . . in private or in the life of society":

> The church gathers to praise God, to hear God's word for humankind, to baptize and to join in the Lord's Supper, to pray for and present the world to God in worship, to enjoy fellowship, to receive instruction, strength, and comfort, to order and organize its own corporate life, to be tested, renewed, and reformed, and to speak and act in the world's affairs as may be appropriate to the needs of the time.

The church disperses to serve God wherever its members are, at work or play, in private or in the life of society. Their prayer and Bible study are part of the church's worship and theological reflection. Their witness is the church's evangelism. Their daily action in the world is the church in mission to the world. The quality of their relation with other persons is the measure of the church's fidelity.

The church I knew, the church of my childhood, was always gathering, always inhaling. I had no experience of full respiration, inhaling and exhaling, which is essential for normal, healthy life. So, the Confession of 1967 gave me the vocabulary I needed to begin thinking about mission in the context of a neighborhood church.

When I first started thinking about this in the 1990s, the language of the "missional church" was not yet in use. Darrell Guder's landmark book, *Missional Church*, had not yet been published. And so I didn't know how to describe precisely what I had in mind. What I had instead was the sense that the churches I served would be healthier if we breathed, if we thought about church life as gathering and dispersing, if we occasionally thought about people other than ourselves. What would come later, as the missional church language became second nature to me, was to think of the church as sending all the time, sending daily, sending minute by minute.

THE MISSION BUDGET AT THE FIRST PRESBYTERIAN CHURCH in Wheaton wasn't small, but it wasn't nearly as large as it could and should have been. We were doing what most churches were doing at the time—namely, supporting what we thought of as "worthy causes" by writing checks, keeping our distance from the need, and then feeling good about our generosity. In other words, mission as most people defined it then. Nothing about our giving had a sense of urgency or immediacy or sacrifice. Few people were directly involved, except for the occasional membership on the board of a nonprofit.

When giving to the church's budget went down, the first line item in the budget to be reduced was mission. The priority was always to pay the staff and the utility bill, and I suppose I should be more grateful for that. Only when our own needs were met would we think about those we considered to be "less fortunate"—the hungry, the thirsty, the naked, the sick, and so on. Further, I remember that when elders were asked about their preferences for committee work, the mission committee was seldom listed as their first choice. The only meaningful power in the church was in the finance committee, and so that was always the most coveted committee assignment (especially among male elders).

I wanted to change all of that. But where to start?

As it turns out, we had our opportunity during my very first year, and the actions we took set the tone for the next decade.

At the end of my first year, First Presbyterian Church showed a budget surplus of $50,000. That hadn't happened before in my ministry, and it never happened again, but we did something in response to it that I still think of as remarkable. We decided to give it away. All of it. There is always a temptation in the church to establish a "rainy day fund," and I seem to remember a few longtime members who counseled against our decision. But the feeling was overwhelming among the church's leadership that we should do something bold, that we should make a statement.

And so, we gave half of the surplus to a nearby overnight shelter, inviting the executive director one Sunday to receive an oversized check for $25,000, and the rest was given away in smaller grants to a list of local and global missions. I cringe as I think about the self-congratulations involved in the larger gift, but I believe that an important tone was set about the priority of mission. The statement we were making—mainly to ourselves—was that we were no longer going to be a grant-making institution, but rather a people who took a personal interest in those who were doing the work of the church in our community (and around the world).

But personal involvement in mission really began with our youth.

YOUTH MISSION TRIPS BECAME A STAPLE OF youth ministry around the country about this time, and my church in Wheaton went all in—not so much because of the gospel mandate I mentioned, but because we were invested in our youth. Throughout the 1990s we sent hundreds of youth every summer to places like West Virginia, Arkansas, Minnesota (the Red Lake Indian Reservation), Wyoming (the Wind River Indian Reservation), and more. We partnered with national organizations that organized the work projects, provided housing, and cooked the meals. The Wheaton church always had the largest group of youth in any camp, and the best dressed too. Where some churches would send a leader (or two), a few youth, and a twelve-passenger van with the church's name on its front door panels, the church in Wheaton would arrive with dozens of youth, a large group of leaders, and a couple of air-conditioned luxury coaches. I am not making this up.

I participated in all of these weeklong trips and have all good memories of the experience, except for occasional embarrassment over the obvious wealth of our church. And, of course, dislike for the sleeping arrangements. Getting to know the youth of the church is easy when you're camped out (boys in one room, girls in another) on the floor of a classroom at a school near the work site. Leaders and youth would spend twenty-four hours a day together. There was never any privacy, not a single moment to get away. We ate our meals in a dining hall, we attended worship gatherings every evening in a school gym, and during free time we played basketball or waited in line at the pay phone to call home. (It's hard to imagine but there was a time before mobile phones.)

These were life-changing experiences for our youth, as well as for most of the adult leaders. When our graduating seniors spoke to the congregation during worship about their fondest memories of church life, the mission trip was always the first one they mentioned. I worry that many of our youth forgot the lessons they learned soon after they arrived at their college campuses, but I remain hopeful that something was retained. They had grown up in a suburb without poverty, but on our mission trips they were forced to see how many people in their own country live. Even with all the justifiable criticism now directed at short-term mission trips, I continue to believe that Christian people from American suburbs will not understand income disparities or the reality of poverty in our country until they are encouraged, however briefly, to see it and, more importantly, spend time with the people who live their lives in it.

The work we did—painting houses, building wheelchair ramps, and making minor home repairs—was not permanent and did not lift anyone out of poverty. A newly painted house must be painted again. Wheelchair ramps do not last more than a few years. I understand all of that, and I find the criticisms of short-term mission trips to be largely valid. I worry that short-term mission trips turn poverty into a spectacle to be observed. An effective solution to the poverty in poor neighborhoods will require far more than a weeklong visit from the high school youth in an affluent Chicago suburb. I understand all of that, but for us, for our church, the mission trips were a way to begin looking beyond ourselves, to begin practicing the life to which Jesus called his followers.

The goal for mission-giving at the Wheaton church, a goal we never reached, but a goal that seemed to attract some energy and excitement, was what we called the "dollar for dollar" goal. When we thought the best thoughts about ourselves, this is who we imagined ourselves to be: For every dollar we spent on ourselves, we would commit to spending a dollar on others. It was ambitious, of course, but we had heard of other churches that had adopted a similar goal and had achieved it. We aspired to be the same kind of high achievers.

Our plan was to begin with a mission budget of ten percent—in other words, ten percent of the annual budget. Ten percent of what the church spent would always be for work beyond our church's own staff, buildings, and programs. And then, we committed to raising the percentage each year until we reached fifty percent of the budget. In the 1990s, with the stock markets reaching new highs every day, the goal seemed ambitious but attainable. However, by the time I left the Wheaton church in 2008, just before the Great Recession, I think the church may have reached a grand total of thirteen percent.

Another of our goals was "hands-on mission"—for every member to participate in mission in a hands-on and personal way. Do something, we would say to new member classes, to grow in your faith, and then do something to give yourself away in faith. In other words, inhaling and exhaling. I think we were more successful at encouraging this kind of behavior than we were with our budget-related goal.

THE ONLY ADULT MISSION TRIP during my years in Wheaton was a trip to Israel, to a school (K–12) in Galilee for Christian, Muslim, Jewish, and Druze children, founded by a Palestinian Christian pastor, Elias Chacour, who later became archbishop of Galilee.

The work we did there might have been done better by local contractors. We painted classrooms, we cleaned, and we planted olive trees, but we also gained a better sense of what life is like for Arab Christians in Israel. We saw firsthand what peacemaking looks like in a region that has known a great deal of war and unrest. We met and came to know people who were very different from us in some significant ways, but very much like us in others. We even received a last-minute invitation to a wedding reception, something that most likely would not have happened if a group of Palestinian Christians had traveled to the United States. One of the group members later became head of a fundraising organization for the school and made several trips back to the school over the next several years. In other words, a relationship was established. A connection was made. The school's founder made several visits to our church in Wheaton and was a guest in my home, as I had been in his.

The church I served after Wheaton was the First Presbyterian Church of Ann Arbor, Michigan, a two-hour drive from my hometown, but a world away in nearly every other respect. That church was directly adjacent to the downtown campus of the University of

Michigan, set between a large fraternity and sorority house. Before my arrival, the church had already been responding to a missional impulse, including but also well beyond the obvious mission field represented by the university campus.

In Haiti, the poorest country in the western hemisphere, the Ann Arbor church helped to establish a nursing school near Leogane. In partnership with the Episcopal church in Haiti and the Hospital Saint Croix in Leogane, the school was (and still is) the only four-year school of nursing in Haiti. A Haitian-born nurse from Miami, Hilda Alcindor, became the school's first dean, and the building was designed by volunteer architects from the University of Michigan. (The design and construction were so good that the school not only survived the 2010 earthquake, which had its epicenter in Leogane, but served as an emergency field hospital for groups like Doctors without Borders in the weeks following the earthquake. Many of the other buildings, including a part of the hospital, collapsed or pancaked, which contributed to the great loss of life during the earthquake and after.) The church's role included providing financial support, establishing a foundation, and coordinating teams of volunteers from the schools of medicine, nursing, and pharmacy at the University of Michigan.

I was proud of this work but often had little to do with it other than offering my support and encouragement.

In 1999, Jimmy Carter and his wife, Rosalynn, led one of his annual building blitzes to the Philippines, to a community near Dumaguete City, and several Ann Arbor church members participated, along with 13,000 other volunteers from thirty-two countries. Because the building blitz was a success and went beyond the original goal of 250 new houses, a new goal was set, and the First Presbyterian Church of Ann Arbor committed itself to returning every year in order to meet that new goal. Later, a dental clinic was also established near the housing development, and dentists affiliated with the University of Michigan School of Dentistry volunteered their time.

I was impressed by the long-term commitment on the part of the church and was encouraged by another form of outreach. Ann Arbor dentists made contact with dentists in and around Dumaguete City and tried to engage them in conversation about giving their time without pay to the residents of the new Jimmy Carter neighborhood (which is the name the community adopted for itself). These conversations were not easy and were not immediately productive, but the work of engaging with Christians and professionals across cultural barriers was worthwhile and mutually instructive.

Finally, the church in Ann Arbor, during my time there, partnered with Presbyterians in Peru to assist at a community center in Huanta, in the central highlands of Peru. Our mission partner was Pedro Arana Quiroz, a Peruvian church leader. The mission in Huanta followed years of fighting in the area, involving both the Peruvian army and members of the Marxist guerrilla group known as the Shining Path. Because of the conflict, few young men dared to stay in the area, and the community center served the women and children who were left in serious need.

The good news about my years in Ann Arbor is that no one needed to be persuaded to engage in the work of mission, except perhaps to strengthen its existing outreach to the nearby campus. The missional impulse was well-developed. We were good at exhaling, though I sometimes wondered about our inhaling.

THE FIRST PRESBYTERIAN CHURCH of Fort Lauderdale, where I landed next, had once again a distinctive history regarding mission. To put it generously, the missional impulse was not well-developed. Though there was a staff member who was deeply engaged in local mission on behalf of the church, and though several members were actively involved in the local Habitat for Humanity, the work of mission, as it had been in Wheaton, was largely a matter of writing checks to worthy causes. Church members themselves seemed disengaged, except for the weekend before Thanksgiving.

Every year, with a list provided by a local government agency, the church provided Thanksgiving dinners to a few hundred families, whose names were provided by the county's Office of Human Services. The groceries were donated by area groceries, and then the food was sorted and boxed in the church's fellowship hall and distributed by members. There was more energy and excitement around mission during this one weekend of the year than at any other time.

Fort Lauderdale and a neighboring community known as Wilton Manors had one of the largest gay populations in the country, but the church itself had no sense of what its mission to that population might mean. At a visioning meeting one Saturday morning, facilitated by a staff member of the Alban Institute, church leaders initially identified "a more diverse church" as a worthy goal, but the facilitator gently pushed back, saying, "Do you know what would be required to do this?" She never said exactly what would be required, but the implication was that *something* would be required, perhaps something big. And that was apparently frightening enough that the leaders quickly dropped diversity as a goal for our church.

With a few more nudges, I had the feeling that Presbyterians in Fort Lauderdale had the potential to be a center and model for mission in south Florida. There was money, after all, but there was also a population of active retirees who wanted to give of themselves. They seemed to need little except direction.

We Had Hoped

Those who love their dream of a Christian community more than the Christian community itself become destroyers of that Christian community even though their personal intentions may be ever so honest, earnest, and sacrificial.

Dietrich Bonhoeffer, *Life Together*

Scratch any cynic and you will find a disappointed idealist.

George Carlin

W. Frank Harrington was once the commencement speaker at a Princeton Seminary graduation, not because he was a Princeton graduate (he wasn't), but because he was pastor of the largest Presbyterian church in the country, the Peachtree Presbyterian Church in Atlanta, Georgia. Peachtree had fewer than 3,000 members when he became pastor, and the church grew to more than 11,000 by the time he died in 1999, of a heart attack at the age of sixty-three.

Harrington was another in a pantheon of white male pastors whom my classmates (the white male classmates) were encouraged to respect, admire, and emulate. I might have learned more from a commencement address given by the pastor of the smallest Presbyterian church in the country, but success was nearly always defined for us in far different terms—size, wealth, prestige, power, and of course whiteness and maleness.

I forget now why I was there that day. I once served a church that was seven miles from the seminary campus, so I may have driven over to see and hear the legendary pastor of the Peachtree Presbyterian Church. I remember a surprising amount of what he said.

What I remember most clearly was the energy and passion he told us that he brought to his work. On Mondays, for example, when most other pastors were sleeping in, taking a day off, and observing a Sabbath, his staff prepared for him a list of every person who had visited his church for the first time the previous day, and then Harrington personally called each one to offer a welcome and to express the hope that they would return. Some pastors, we were told, hand off this assignment to a staff member or, worse, to a volunteer, or else they wait to follow up until later in the week. But follow up with visitors is far too important for that, Harrington told us. Church shoppers will have made up their minds to go elsewhere by Wednesday, he said, citing a recent study on the matter.

I knew as soon as I heard that story that I would be spending my Mondays on the telephone. Instead of being concerned about Harrington's marriage and family, and of course his spiritual and physical health, what I thought during that graduation ceremony was that I must not be working hard enough. I started out after ordination determined to take a day off each week, but I soon realized that the pastors who were succeeding didn't seem to need a day off. I remember thinking that I needed to step up my game.

Harrington said something else that I have not forgotten: "As far as I'm concerned," he declared, "I still hear trumpets in the morning!" I forget, but the title of his address may have included those words: "trumpets in the morning." Every single morning he heard trumpets summoning him to work.

I have heard trumpets in the morning a few times too, but I don't hear them *every* morning. I have felt and even in retirement feel a strong sense of calling in my work, as though I have been summoned, but do I wake up each morning to a trumpet fanfare? The short answer is no, and even now I feel a twinge of guilt about admitting that, as though something must be wrong with me.

Over the years I brought a great deal of energy and passion to my work. I seem to have been blessed with more stamina than many people. I look nothing like a long-distance runner but somehow was able to run several marathons after my fortieth birthday. At least three, and often four, nights per week at the church were not uncommon for much of my ministry, and like most pastors I worked every weekend and major holiday. I tried to keep work hours to no more than sixty per week, but in peak seasons of the year, like Advent and Lent, my work hours easily crept toward eighty. Presbyterian pastors receive a standard of four weeks of vacation each year, which is generous, but most years I didn't use all four. I remember hearing from another large church pastor that being away from my church more than two

Sundays in a row was a bad idea. I now forget the study that supported this view. Besides, he said, there were many people shopping for a church in August, just prior the beginning of the school year. So, after two weeks at the lake with my family in July, I was always ready to get back to work, to welcome those church shoppers, and of course to be as successful as I could be.

I do not write this to ask for sympathy; I write this to confess my foolishness. No one ever asked me, in so many words, to attend all of those evening meetings. No one ever said that I shouldn't use all of my vacation days. No one ever thanked me for preaching all of those summer Sundays in August. In fact, I remember being angry at one point that no one was watching out for me, that someone on the personnel committee, for example, didn't take me aside and tell me to ease off a little. Too late I realized that I was expected to take care of myself.

To be fair to Princeton Seminary, not all of the commencement speakers were large church pastors. The Dutch priest and theologian Henri Nouwen was once invited to give the commencement address, as was the Presbyterian pastor Eugene Peterson. For twenty-five years Peterson was the founding pastor of a relatively small new church development in Bel Air, Maryland, before leaving to become a professor at Regent College in Vancouver. He wrote extensively about the spiritual life and about being a pastor, and I had read most of his books. I liked the idea that he was a pastor who found time to write. His church never grew to more than two or three hundred members—a red flag, I suppose—but he was white and male and a published author, so Princeton invited him to speak.

When Peterson's name was announced as that year's commencement speaker, I wrote and invited him to preach the day after the graduation at the church I was serving in Hopewell, New Jersey. To my surprise he accepted my invitation and not the invitation to a much larger Presbyterian church in Princeton, closer to the seminary.

I was thrilled. I should have paid more attention to what he wrote about being a pastor. I know from his writing that he did not spend his Mondays telephoning visitors.

FOR TEN YEARS, EARLY IN MY CAREER, I was editor of the *General Assembly News* (once called the *General Assembly Daily News*) a tabloid-sized newspaper, published each day during what were, at the time, annual meetings of the national deliberative body of the Presbyterian Church (USA). There was also a twelve-page "wrap-up edition" published at the conclusion of each Assembly and mailed to every pastor in the Presbyterian Church.

I spent at least ten days each year at the site of these meetings—in places like Minneapolis, Salt Lake City, Phoenix, St. Louis, and Biloxi—stayed at a fine downtown hotel, made use of a generous per diem for meals, and had the use of a rental car (to drive from the convention center to the printer and back).

Each General Assembly meeting had a newsroom where a team of volunteer reporters prepared news releases and where the newsroom manager assigned stories and met with national and local media to explain the sometimes-arcane language used at Assembly meetings. The first newsroom manager I worked with was something of a legend in the Presbyterian Church. He came to church work from a small-town newspaper in New Mexico and always spoke with a salty wit and wisdom. Vic Jameson worked in the Presbyterian Office of Information for more than thirty years, and after the northern and southern streams of the Presbyterian Church reunited in 1984, he moved to Atlanta where he became editor of the denominational magazine, *Presbyterian Survey*. Somehow, he was fiercely devoted to the church while maintaining a critical distance, which I admired.

Jameson was my boss, and though his decisions were always final, I worked with what seems now like a surprising amount of independence. If he didn't like something I had done, he would circle the offending words (or headline) with a red marker and write "see me."

I kept late hours, often working at the printing company until two or three o'clock in the morning, and I wouldn't get to the newsroom until late morning. I dreaded seeing that morning's marked-up newspaper waiting for me on my desk. He kept inviting me back each year, though, so he must have liked my work. Mostly I enjoyed doing it.

According to one newsroom legend, my predecessor in the position wrote a headline for the front page, above the fold, which was relatively benign: "Stated Clerk Andrews Announces Shift in Administration." But, as a prank, mainly directed at Jameson, my predecessor convinced the printer to print a few copies of the paper with the letter "f" missing from the word "shift." The prank edition was distributed only in the newsroom the next morning, and everyone waited for Jameson's reaction. Apparently, there were several seconds of anguished silence while Jameson sat at his desk and stared at the front page. Finally, to everyone's relief, he burst into laughter. Similar prank editions were produced every year after that.

The most exciting year during my years as editor was 1984 when the northern and southern churches, the UPCUSA and the PCUS, joined together after more than a hundred years of division and several difficult years of negotiating a reunion. The joining together of the two General Assemblies happened in Atlanta, and the headline in the *General Assembly News*, in the largest type size I had ever used, was "We Are One Church Again!" More than one person felt compelled to tell me that a truly united church was more of an eschatological hope than a present reality; still, the intentions and celebrations at the time seemed genuine. Whatever joy we felt, though, was short-lived.

The reunited church in 1984 claimed more than 3.1 million members. By 2018, the reunited church, the PCUSA, claimed a little more than 1.3 million members. The decline that had begun years earlier (in north and south) continued unabated.

WHEN I FIRST TOOK THE JOB AS EDITOR, I remember thinking that it was a way to keep my hand in the publishing business, in case my career in the church didn't work out. Beginning with my work on the college newspaper, and then my summer employment at Eerdmans, I had always considered writing, editing, and publishing a possible career path and continued to think about that even after ordination. When I finally let go of the *General Assembly News*, I was letting go of what I had always considered to be a lifeline, if I needed it.

At first, I found these annual meetings of the church to be fascinating, and I approached them with childlike wonder. I met many people I had previously only read about, and I was more impressed than I should have been to meet so many seminary presidents, theologians, national church leaders, and of course large church pastors who always seemed to attend these meetings, whether or not they had any official role to play.

One of my seminary classmates, who was always angling for a new and better job in the church, would arrive early at the hotel closest to the convention center, check into a hospitality suite, and then set up a bar with a surprisingly large and varied assortment of alcohol. Evenings in the hotel suite, after a day of deliberations, were a time to meet, relax, gossip, and whisper about business on the Assembly floor. At the first one of these gatherings I ever attended, I made the connection I needed to get the job as editor of the *General Assembly News*. I was quite impressed by all of this at the time, but after a couple of years, I lost my enthusiasm and stopped going altogether.

Commissioners to General Assembly meetings, chosen from among the pastors and elders in each presbytery (or regional governing body), always came back from these meetings with glowing reports about their work, and the truth is that they put in long hours and debated weighty issues. They enjoyed the worship, found the debates exciting, and enjoyed serving their church at the national level.

At the beginning I felt the same way. As the years went by, though, I found less and less enjoyment in the meetings. I tired of meeting church leaders. I no longer looked forward to hearing seminary presidents talk at length about their schools. I even grew weary of walking through the exhibit hall where publishers and church supply companies hawked their wares. Plastic communion cups? Liturgical stoles for each season of the church year? Offering envelopes decorated with religious art? You could find all of it there—and more!

Each year the commissioners learned from the stated clerk's report that the church was declining. Membership, worship attendance, giving, baptisms, and confirmations were all down, sometimes by startling amounts. And yet commissioners would speak so earnestly in debate. "The eyes of the world are on us," they would sometimes say, especially if a motion about same-sex ordination was being debated, but as I listened I decided that the eyes of the world were most likely not on us, not on our debate, and not on anything we had to say. I would sit in the gallery, with hundreds of other spectators, and think about how little meaning these decisions and declarations and pronouncements had.

A decision to disinvest in US corporations doing business with Israel might be considered national news—and the newsroom would be crowded with reporters from both national and local media outlets to learn more about it—but the news had little long-term significance. I would return to my church, and my church members would quiz me about headlines they had seen. And then, soon after, the matter faded from their consciousness.

Faced with budget cuts, the General Assembly made the difficult decision to meet only once every two years, rather than every year. I heard few complaints about not meeting as often.

Curiously, I first noticed my disillusionment with the church when I was serving the church in Wheaton. In other words, as I was enjoying the largest membership growth of any church I have ever served, as money seemed to appear without much effort, and as the building and staff expanded, I became aware that something wasn't right. I wouldn't be able to name what was happening to me for a few more years, but it seems clear now that I was becoming more and more disillusioned. What I had devoted my life to, what I was willing to give so much of my time and energy to, what I had given up a career as a writer and editor to do, turned out to be an illusion. I started to think of these national meetings and all of the posturing and politicking as empty and without meaning.

"Chasing after wind" was how my grandmother would have described it, echoing the words of Ecclesiastes. The church was not what I hoped it would be. What I thought I wanted was not what I wanted at all.

DISILLUSIONMENT HAS ALWAYS SEEMED TO ME to be a negative thing, and for a long time that's how I experienced it. Which is why I have been surprised recently to find writers about the spiritual life describing disillusionment as a positive thing, perhaps even a gift. Barbara Brown Taylor, in her sermon collection titled *God in Pain*, writes that, while disillusionment can be painful, it is never bad. When we find ourselves "disillusioned," she writes, "we find out what is not true and we are set free to seek what is—if we dare—to turn away from the God who was supposed to be in order to seek the God who is."

I now see, of course, that this is true, and I find myself wishing that I had allowed myself to be disillusioned much earlier in my life and in my work. If I had seen clearly at the beginning, I might have dared, in Taylor's language, to turn away from one way of being a pastor in order to seek a different way, a healthier and more authentic way.

In a recent sermon, Nadia Bolz-Weber said that the three words spoken by Jesus's disciples on the road to Emmaus— "we had hoped"—are "among the saddest words in all of scripture." The setting is Luke 24, and the time is late on Easter day. Two disciples, having followed Jesus, having devoted their lives to him, having risked everything, were now returning to Emmaus, their hopes crushed. A stranger, we are told, joined them as they walked, and improbably they did not recognize him as Jesus.

He asked them to explain what they were talking about, and Cleopas, one of the two, responded, "Are you the only stranger in Jerusalem who does not know the things that have taken place in these days?" To keep them talking, Jesus said, "What things?" So, they said, "The things about Jesus of Nazareth, who was a prophet mighty in deed and word before God and all the people."

At this point, we hear the sad summary of their disillusionment: "We had hoped that he was the one to redeem Israel."

I find myself joining them at that moment and saying, "I had hoped for a few things, too. I had hoped that the church would grow as it did when I was a child. I had hoped that the church would turn out to be a source of grace as it had been for me in Iowa City all those years ago. I had hoped that my work would mostly be to tell others about that grace."

But nearly twenty years into my life and work as a pastor I realized that what I had hoped was an illusion, a fiction. The church I had hoped for has probably never existed, except in brief moments over the years, like that moment in my own life when I made the wonderful discovery that I was loved unconditionally. Most of the time, the church is imperfect and fallen and prone to be disappointing.

In his book *Life Together*, Dietrich Bonhoeffer warns of the damage caused by unrealistic expectations of life in the church: "Certainly, serious Christians who are put in a community for the first time will often bring with them a very definite image of what Christian communal life should be, and they will be anxious to realize it. But God's grace quickly frustrates all such dreams. A great disillusionment with others, with Christians in general, and if we are fortunate, with ourselves is bound to overwhelm us, as surely as God desires to lead us to an understanding of Christian community."

If we are fortunate!

How is it that I have given forty years of my life to this work and now, at long last, see things for what they are? Disillusionment is a gift, maybe, but it is a painful gift. I suppose it is God who shatters and dismantles our illusions. I suppose it is God who lays waste to our foolishness, our careerism, and our self-importance. I suppose it is God who allows us to be humbled, so that we can see at last what is real and what is of lasting importance.

I told myself that I was following the way of the cross, and what I found was that I was following the way of success as American culture defines it.

13

Lunch at the Golden Nugget

I still encourage anyone who feels at all compelled to write to do so. I just try to warn people who hope to get published that publication is not all it is cracked up to be. But writing is.

Anne Lamott, *Bird by Bird:
Some Instructions on Writing and Life*

I've developed a great reputation for wisdom by ordering more books than I ever had time to read, and reading more books, by far, than I learned anything useful from, except, of course, that some very tedious gentlemen have written books.

Marilynne Robinson, *Gilead*

My first book tour consisted of speaking engagements and book signings at churches in Fort Wayne, Toledo, and Las Vegas—a mixed bag. The promotional tour for my second book consisted of an appearance on a Christian cable TV show, broadcast from a small town in Indiana and hosted by a former Miss America, who was very pretty. When my third book was published, the church secretary decided, after a week or two, that the thing had been displayed on the reception desk in the church office "long enough" and moved them "out of the way" to a nearby closet. It was not the career trajectory as an author that I had dreamed about.

But writing was what I wanted to do for as long as I can remember, ever since I realized that I could express myself by putting a few words on a page. I started to practice writing on my own in junior high by buying spiral notebooks and trying out different styles. One time, for an entire summer, I wrote about myself in the third person, because that was what Norman Mailer did in his book *Of a Fire on the Moon*, an account of the first moon landing. Mailer referred to himself there as "Aquarius," so for a summer I became "Scorpio," a literary device that worked better for Mailer than it did for me, though not by much. I also wrote quite a few sports columns that no one but me ever saw, and I thought for a while that being paid to watch baseball games and write about them might be an ideal career.

I was first a sports editor and then later an associate editor for my high school newspaper, *Courtviews*. During my college years, I was first a staff writer and then later an associate editor for my college newspaper, *Chimes*. Somewhere between high school and college newspapers I contributed to something called the "Youth Page," which appeared every Saturday in the *Grand Rapids Press*. My parents were embarrassed about a profile I wrote one time about a man who played piano in a bar. They were always worried that my writing would embarrass them.

My experience with the college newspaper was a personal triumph for me because of the paper's storied history. Peter DeVries, a novelist and staff writer for the *New Yorker*, was a *Chimes* editor in 1931. His escape from the Christian Reformed Church and from his strict Dutch Calvinist background made him one of my early heroes. I still have most of his novels on a shelf above my desk. In the late 1960s, *Chimes* editorial staff members included Paul Schrader, Jeanine Oppewal, and Bill Brashler, who all went on to careers in writing and filmmaking, with Schrader best known for writing the screenplays for *Taxi Driver* and *Raging Bull*, among others. I had no Hollywood ambitions, but when I was in high school I admired these people for the controversy they created, as much as for the newspaper they produced. And then, Patricia Rozema, who came along after me, was an editor of *Chimes* in 1979 and became a well-known film director in Canada, writing and directing, for example, the 1999 film *Mansfield Park*.

Soon after graduating from seminary I began to contribute short essays to the *Reformed Journal*, a small-circulation magazine with an editorial board I admired. My first essay was titled "Woe Is Me," an honest reflection on my first few months of ordained ministry. I was a contributing editor to the *Reformed Journal* for seven years, and then later to *Perspectives*, its successor journal, for another sixteen.

FEW AUTHORS EVER FORGET THE EXCITEMENT THAT comes from having their first book published. Members at my church in Wheaton organized a book signing at the Borders bookstore in the Rice Lake Square shopping mall. Dozens of church members turned out for the occasion, one of the most thrilling nights of my life.

John Mulder, who had by then left his teaching position at Princeton Seminary to become president at Louisville Presbyterian Theological Seminary, confided to me after my first book was published that I would make more money talking about the book than selling copies of it. And he was right.

Based on the publication of my first book, *Remembering the Faith: What Christians Believe*, I received an invitation to speak at a church in Las Vegas. The visit was unremarkable in most ways because life off the famous Las Vegas strip is surprisingly normal. And since I stayed at the home of a member, the closest I came to the strip was seeing it from a distance on my ride back to the airport. Along the way, we stopped for lunch at the Golden Nugget and ordered the French onion soup, a specialty of Chef Greg, who turned out to be a member of the church and who came out to our table to say hello, decked out of course in his *toque blanche*. Before the meal, my hosts and I held hands and prayed, and as we prayed I heard the sound of slot machines in the background—*ding, ding, ding, ding!* I remember thinking, "This is one of the weirdest things I've ever done."

Book signings were exciting at the beginning and then less so as the months passed. I remember being asked to sign copies of my first book in the exhibit area at a General Assembly meeting. As it turned out, five or six authors were invited to do the same thing at the same time, and for much of the advertised signing period we talked among ourselves, signing few if any books. Presbyterians who were strolling through the exhibit area seemed to look awkwardly in our direction before they hurried away, not knowing, I suppose, what to say to a published author. The Wheaton Religious Gift and Church Supply store, which always supplied my Wheaton church with ashes for our Ash Wednesday service, asked me to sign my book on what turned out to be a beautiful Saturday afternoon, the first after a particularly long and cold winter. I don't remember that a single person stopped by to meet me that day or to buy my book, in spite of what seemed like a pretty good promotional campaign.

The summer after *Remembering the Faith* was published, I took a copy along on my family vacation. My family went to the same beach association every summer, and I came to know a retired pastor from another denomination who lived there year-round. Each year, after we were settled into our rental, he would pedal his bike over and talk with me about the church. Mostly he would complain about young pastors who didn't call on members in their homes as much as they should. The church, in his estimation, had been going downhill ever since he retired. Even so, I was proud to hand over a copy of my book as a gift to him. I remember that he took it, eyed it suspiciously, and then said, "Well, I'm glad you got that out of your system," as though my writing was taking me away from the more important work of calling on members in their homes. I never heard another word from him about the book.

WRITING FOR ME HAS BEEN partly a creative activity, like painting or cooking. I enjoy the challenge of expressing ideas in clever and sometimes humorous ways, but always in what I thought were the best ways. My favorite preachers have always been those who use language well. I admire their craftsmanship. Similarly, I have always disliked preachers who give little evidence of reading, who never seem to give a thought to how their words sound when spoken aloud. I tried not to be one of those preachers, though my concern over the way my words looked on the page probably kept me from being a better preacher than I was. Speaking and writing, after all, are two different kinds of communication. Being good at one doesn't always mean being good at the other, though there are exceptions.

But writing has also been for me a way to figure things out for myself. My second book, *Beyond "I Do": What Christians Believe about Marriage*, was my attempt to understand what marriage is. I had been caught up for years in the wedding industrial complex, officiating at dozens of weddings each year, many of them elaborate and expensive affairs, and I began to wonder what my role amounted to. Bookshelves are filled with books about how to make marriages better, so another self-help book wasn't needed. What *was* needed, I thought, was another look at marriage from a biblical and theological point of view. So I reviewed marriage's history, especially the role that the church has played over the centuries. I looked carefully (for the first time in my life) at what the Bible actually said about marriage—which is surprisingly little given the importance most contemporary believers attach to the subject. And, finally, I reflected on changes that have been occurring within marriage because of recent changes within culture.

As with my first book, my book about marriage grew out of an adult class I taught at the Wheaton church. I realized that I was never going to write a book unless I found a way to make it grow out of my work. The class (and later the book) addressed issues like covenant and sacrament as the theological foundations for marriage. (I argued that while marriage is not a sacrament in Protestant churches, it is nevertheless sacramental, which was news to me.) The class was surprisingly well-received and even ended with a ceremony for renewing wedding vows, an unexpected and satisfying outcome to the class. One woman, I won't forget, proudly wore her wedding dress for the occasion.

Though the class (and book) addressed singleness, I could have done a better job of looking at a broader range of human relationships. But given the suburban setting and my church's almost single-minded focus on family units, I kept my own focus narrow. I also addressed same-sex relationships in the class and invited a friend who teaches Old Testament at a Methodist seminary to explore relevant biblical texts. This particular class session, not surprisingly, had the highest attendance of any in the series. I taught in the sanctuary, and on this particular day the lower level was nearly filled with well over two hundred people. Church members who were not a part of previous classes obviously made a point of attending this one. When my friend, Tom Dozeman, was finished with the biblical texts that are frequently cited in connection with homosexuality, someone in the front row raised a hand and said, "Yes, but what do *you* believe?"

I have always liked to give church members the tools and information they need to form their own opinions, but in the culture wars of the last few decades taking sides is sometimes more important than coming to well-formed opinions. With this in mind, I deliberately omitted the chapter on same-sex relationships from my book, hoping that the book would reach a wider audience, especially among evangelical readers. I now regret having done so. Leaving it out was cowardly. My concern for church unity has always trumped my willingness to say clearly what I believed. My friend Tom had no such hesitation. To the person who wanted to know what he believed, he said simply, "It's not an issue for me."

Curiously, the most controversial topic from the classes and sermons that turned into my first book was the resurrection—not Jesus's, but ours, what the Apostles' Creed calls the "resurrection of the body."

As a pastor I should have known that this topic would touch a nerve. I have officiated at enough funerals over the years to know that people wanted to hear—in some cases *needed* to hear—that their loved one was now safely in the arms of God. Except that the Bible doesn't say that exactly. Teachings about life after death aren't a prominent feature of Judaism because the Hebrew Bible has little to say about life after death. The New Testament isn't necessarily more helpful. It's true that Jesus told the thief on the cross that "today you will be with me in paradise." But elsewhere there is the suggestion that the dead will sleep—what the apostle Paul puzzlingly refers to as "soul sleep"—until the final resurrection when all will be raised together. Grieving people aren't comforted when they're told that the person they loved is off sleeping somewhere.

Overall my sermon series and adult classes on basic Christian doctrine were well received. Worship attendance actually *increased* over the seventeen weeks, which is counterintuitive considering the topic. But the sermon and class about life after death was the most controversial of the series, and I dropped it from the book. One reviewer, to his credit, noticed the omission and commented about it. I should have left it in.

ONE OF MY FAVORITE WRITERS over the years has been Marilynne Robinson, especially her series of novels set in the fictional Iowa town she calls Gilead. What I like about Robinson isn't only what she writes, but how she writes it. Her use of language can be breathtaking.

I taught an adult class on Robinson's first novel in the Gilead series at my Ann Arbor church. My plan was to team teach with John Whittier-Ferguson, a church member and University of Michigan English professor. He was going to address the language in the text while I explained the theological themes, which at the beginning seemed like a sound approach. At some point during the first class, though, I found myself taking a seat in the first row, so that I could listen to my friend, the English professor. He would read a paragraph or two, coming close to tears over the beauty of Robinson's language, and then he would explain to us why the words were so beautiful. As it turned out, he knew all the theology he needed to know.

Early in my career, I enjoyed reading Eugene Peterson's books. I enjoyed them so much that I invited him to preach for me, as I described in the previous chapter. Peterson introduced his congregation to a pastor-scholar model of ministry. He spent most summers on a lake in Montana, where he was from, and he wrote. I was jealous and once asked my Wheaton church for a three-month summer sabbatical. I even applied for a Lilly Endowment grant to write what became my second book. The personnel committee was not immediately enthusiastic about the plan. There was nothing in the personnel manual, after all, about sabbaticals or leaves of absence, and I heard the usual protests about how sabbaticals were really for people in academic careers. Most church members were in business or law and found the idea of getting away to think, study, and write to be odd and, frankly, lazy. I persisted, though, and was finally given permission to go. I even took the sabbatical at a time when it would have the least impact on church life.

With the Lilly money, I was able to take my family to Europe in 1990, mainly to Italy. Since I'm an early riser, I would write for a few hours each morning, and then (when my teenage daughters were awake) we would set off for a day of sight-seeing. We lived for a week at a time in various locations and used that location as a hub for exploring. In spite of the cathedrals, museums, Roman ruins, and natural beauty of Italy, my daughters still think of our brief stop in Salzburg, Austria, as the high point of the trip. It was there that we were able to take a *The Sound of Music* bus tour, visiting all of the places where the famous movie was made.

I came back from my sabbatical with so much energy that one of the church leaders said to me, "If we had known what the sabbatical would do for you, we would have suggested it years ago," as though it had been the church's idea all along. But it was true, the time and distance helped me to recharge and return to work with new energy. All pastors, even those who have no interest in writing, should take regular breaks from their work. My three-month sabbatical, though, was the only sabbatical I took in forty years of ministry.

Frederick Buechner is still another writer who has had an impact on my life, in large part because he is also a Presbyterian pastor. I never liked his novels, but I devoured his nonfiction. He was always a great source of quotes for an older generation of preachers—my generation. I still think his sermon about Jacob wrestling with an angel, "The Magnificent Defeat," is one of the best pieces of religious writing I have ever read.

I never heard Buechner preach, and it's possible I would have been disappointed if I had. Buechner's language was intended to be read, not heard. Early in my ministry, I wanted to think of myself as someone who had been ordained to write, as someone who was ordained to the ministry of writing. I always thought that writing would allow me to reach a larger audience. Even though Buechner never served a church, he served a large congregation—one that included me.

He was also one of the first writers I knew who wrote movingly about personal issues. And by writing about them, he seemed more approachable, human, and authentic. Just about everybody writes about personal issues these days, and so it might be hard to believe that it was once rare, but it was, especially for pastors. In his book *Telling Secrets*, Buechner wrote for the first time about how his alcoholic father killed himself by breathing car exhaust when Buechner was just ten years old. His mother insisted that Buechner and his brother keep the suicide a secret, and he did until one day at midlife he found himself in a psychiatrist's office and began exploring the toll that his silence had taken on him. "Death," he wrote, "had ended my father, but it had never ended my relationship with my father."

The other "secret" in the book was his daughter's struggle with anorexia. The idea that a pastor's family could have such a serious struggle was not new, but Buechner wrote about his "secrets" with such care and tenderness and feeling that readers were given permission to explore their own "secrets."

I have been told many times over the years that my sermons are "so honest," that the feelings I share and the stories I tell are unexpectedly real. No one has ever told me that my sermons are *too* honest, and I aim for a healthy amount of self-disclosure, but I find it hard to understand how preaching cannot be honest, how preaching cannot explore disappointments and failures and humiliations. In *Telling Secrets*, Buechner writes, "In these pages I tell secrets about my parents, my children, [and] myself . . . because that is not only more honest but also vastly more interesting than to pretend that I have no such secrets to tell."

CHAPTER 13

The secrets I've shared in my writing and in my preaching over the years never seemed all that secret to me. They were the kinds of the things that all people think about—what we fear, how we feel when we fail, and what we dream about. I never thought that any of my honesty was an end itself. For me it was always a way to present my faith in a more authentic way.

14

The Holy Bits

*The shining face of Moses and his need to wear a veil outside of the
sanctuary underscore his permanent separation from the Israelites as
a result of his ordination.*

Thomas B. Dozeman, *Holiness and Ministry:
A Biblical Theology of Ordination*

*Whenever there is stillness there is the still small voice, God's speaking
from the whirlwind, nature's old song, and dance.*

Annie Dillard, *Teaching a Stone to Talk:
Expeditions and Encounters*

I BAPTIZED MY OLDER DAUGHTER, SARAH, when she was three months old. She was not my first baptism, though she was among my first. I was new to the sacraments then. I had only been ordained for a couple of years and hadn't taken the course at seminary on the big, dramatic gestures of worship, which is how the seminary thought of the sacraments (they were taught by a member of the speech department). When I graduated, I had no idea how to take a baby from a parent or how to apply the water or how to do much of anything that ordination allowed me to do.

Happily, though, I worked with an experienced senior pastor, Fred Anderson, who was more than willing to show me. At 6:30 on the Sunday morning before my first baptism, before the minister of music arrived to practice the organ, Fred and I went to the sanctuary with a large baby doll I had stolen from the church nursery, and I practiced holding the baby and administering the water and saying the words I had memorized. There's a higher degree of difficulty involved in all of that than most people realize.

Fred's approach to infant baptism was to take large fistfuls of water from the font and apply them to the baby's head—one fistful each for the Father, and the Son, and the Holy Spirit. Those babies were always in for a soaking. The baptismal liturgy says that in baptism we die to our old selves and rise to new life in Christ, and Fred intended to get those babies as close to a drowning as he could.

Sarah was dressed for her baptism in a long, white baptismal gown that had been in the family for years. A few of her cousins had been baptized while wearing the same gown, and a few more have worn it at their baptisms in the years since. I took Sarah from her mother's arms, having had quite a bit of experience by this point, and then, standing close to the massive stone font, I looked into her eyes, just as I had moments after she was born. I confidently grabbed a fist-ful of water and applied it to her head, and I managed to say, "Sarah DeYoung Brouwer, I baptize you in the name of the Father. . . ." But that was as far as I got. Suddenly, in that moment, I realized where I was and what I was doing, and I was so overwhelmed by it all, the meaning of it, that I was unable to go on.

Fred could see that no more words were going to come out of my mouth, so without hesitation he took over. He grabbed two more fistfuls of water and finished the job: ". . . and of the Son, and of the Holy Spirit. Amen!" He soaked both of us. And that's how Sarah was baptized, a tag-team effort, unusual in the annals of Protestant wor-ship. She was a child of the covenant, sealed in the Spirit, and marked as Christ's own forever. We sang a baptismal hymn that had been written for the occasion, and then it was over.

I don't mind saying that those few minutes were among the high points of my ministry. I was aware in the moment that what had hap-pened was holy, though at the time I would not have been able to say why. In Sarah's baptism, though, I began to understand a bit more clearly what my ordination meant. Ordination, I realized, meant that I would get to spend time with the holy bits, that I would get to lead people to the point where they could experience the holy, if they wanted to. I would be allowed to dip my hand into the waters of baptism, to hold the bread and cup of the Lord's Supper, to pronounce words of blessing on people entering the covenant of marriage, to say words of comfort and hope at times of death, and more. I began to see my ordination first as a great privilege and then, later, as a great responsibility. I realized that my life as a pastor would be filled with holy moments, not just with my family, but with many others, in a variety of settings. In the words of the apostle Paul, I had become "a steward of the mysteries of God," a job description that I never tired of, even when, later in my career, I began to fall out of love with the Presbyterian Church.

Once, on my first pilgrimage to Israel, I led a group of church members from my Wheaton church in worship near the Sea of Galilee. It was our second day in the country, so I may have been jet-lagged, but I am confident that the experience was genuine. There were thirty-one of us gathered in a small chapel, with the lake plainly visible through the large windows, and as their pastor I stood to read scripture and speak briefly.

Suddenly, as with my daughter's baptism several years before, I realized where I was and what I was doing. It was my privilege and responsibility to lead my people to the point where they could experience the holy, if they wanted to. I had heard about Galilee since I was a five-year-old child in Sunday school. Mrs. Peterson, my teacher, made the setting come alive in my imagination so that even then, as a five-year-old, I could see it in my mind's eye. And now here I was, at last, with the responsibility to tell my group what this place meant and why it should matter to them. I cried again, as I did at my daughter's baptism and as I do often in the presence of the holy, but this time I was able to keep going. After spending a few years growing into the role, I knew finally who I was and what I was supposed to be doing in the moment.

FINDING THE HOLY IN BAPTISM isn't all that hard, as it turns out. It's one of those rites within worship where, if you're the least bit open to the holy, you can usually see it or feel it. At other times, and in other places, finding the holy can be much more difficult. At meetings of the buildings and grounds committee, for example, with a group of guys (in my experience they were almost always men) doing nothing more than comparing estimates for roof repairs, God's presence can be somewhat harder to see.

These were never my favorite meetings, and whenever possible I avoided them, but when I was there, I would find myself looking at those men and seeing in them faithful servants of God, doing God's work. Repairing the roof might not seem like God's work, but that's just the point. For me in those moments, if not always for them, carefully examining those estimates, it was clearly God's work. These men would bring all their skill and expertise to fixing a roof, but I could see that they were fixing the tabernacle of God, the place where so much that was holy in their lives occurred—the Christmas pageants of their children and grandchildren, the baptisms and funerals of people they loved, and sometimes weddings, too—perhaps even their own. I could sense all of this as they worked, and I frequently wondered how I could show them what they were doing, what was really going on. In those moments I remembered why I loved to be a pastor.

When I would go the hospital (for pastors "business travel" usually consists of driving to the hospital) and take the elevator to the fifth floor, and then walk down the hall looking for the room where a member of my congregation was lying in a hospital bed, I knew that I was not just anyone who happened to walk in off the street. In these visits I knew, as I did during baptisms and during meetings of the buildings and grounds committee, that I was a Minister of Word and Sacrament.

When the person in the hospital bed saw me and invited me in, she was seeing not just a tall man with a concerned smile. She was seeing her pastor, someone who could be counted on to know God and to be familiar (to some extent) with the ways of God. She was expecting that I would bring with me a worship bulletin from the previous Sunday's service, but also a piece of what happened there, the holiness that her church family had seen and participated in. When I took her hand to pray at the end of the visit, there would be something in the touching of our hands that let her know that she was in the presence of God. I always knew that it was my work to do those things, to be that person, to be mindful of that presence. I never grew tired of visiting church members in the hospital.

Like many pastors I spent too much of my time being a program director for children, youth, college students, singles, families, older adults, recovering divorced people, and all the other niche groups in the life of any church. That's a fine thing to do, or it can be, but I wish I had spent less of my time being that person. I wish I had spent less of my time as a manager and a therapist and a community activist. What I really wanted to be, and what the church really needs, are pastors who are "stewards of the mysteries of God."

MY FRIEND TOM DOZEMAN is an Old Testament scholar who once took up the challenge of the World Council of Churches (WCC). In 1982, in an important paper called "Baptism, Eucharist, and Ministry," the WCC challenged churches to search out the biblical meaning of ordination, partly so that churches around the world would begin talking about it, and partly so that Christians would have a biblical and theological framework for thinking about it.

As an Old Testament scholar, Tom didn't have to search much further than the few chapters in the book of Exodus where he had spent much of his career. His book, *Holiness and Ministry: A Biblical Theology of Ordination*, locates the biblical origins of ordination right at the beginning, in the wilderness of Sinai. Many Christians look to the New Testament for role models—to Peter and (more often) to Paul. But Tom argues that we should look much further back—to the first books of the Bible. As the people of Israel were wandering around the Sinai desert, they were doing important work. They were sorting out for themselves the ways in which they would live with and worship their God. They developed what we might call "holy habits." Basically, they named the holy. They came to understand it, as much as holiness can be understood. They even developed the rituals and created the space and designed the furniture that would allow them to spend time with the holy.

Priests and Levites were the people allowed to touch the holy bits. They were the ones entrusted with the same duties and responsibilities that Ministers of Word and Sacrament are today. Our jobs find their origins in theirs. Priests and Levites were no better than the rest of the people, and they often proved that they weren't, but their work, their calling, was devoted to God's presence and God's interactions with the people. Everyone participated, of course, but it was the priests and Levites who made sure things happened as they were supposed to, even though God occasionally reminded everyone, including priests and Levites, that no building, no piece of furniture, and no sacred ritual could contain the divine presence.

ONCE, AS I WAS ABOUT TO LEAD a family into the church sanctuary for a funeral, an usher who was holding the door for us whispered to me in a confidential tone, "I sure don't envy you having to do this."

It wasn't the moment to have a conversation, and I knew he meant to express his concern for me, but what I would have said in that moment, and before all of the other funerals I have been asked to lead, is this: "I have never felt more like a pastor than right now. This is what I have been trained and equipped to do. It is a great privilege to be invited by a family into their grief, to hear their sobs, and to find the words to say that they are unable to speak. I wouldn't want to be anywhere else but in this holy moment."

The funeral where the usher made a point of whispering to me was a big one. The person who had died was young, someone whose name had been mentioned in worship during prayer concerns for several weeks, someone who had left a husband and young children. To be able to give thanks for the life of an older person is easy by comparison. Services for the young, particularly for children, are always unimaginably difficult.

I remember a brief funeral service for a newborn. It took place in a hospital room and was attended by the parents and a couple of nurses. I remember a service for a teenager who had died of an underlying heart condition while swimming in a lake at summer camp. I remember others, each one painful in its own way. These funerals were some of the most difficult experiences of my ministry, and yet—I also remember each one as a holy moment. They were holy in their intimacy, they were holy in their suffering, they were holy in the sense that there was nowhere else to turn but to something beyond ourselves. Death had brought us together, and it had stripped us of our pride and arrogance and false hope. Death, strangely enough, provided the setting in which we could see and know and experience the holy.

Most people are surprised to hear this, but pastors would overwhelmingly prefer to officiate at a funeral rather than a wedding. At a church wedding, God too often feels like an afterthought, not the reason people gather. A scripture reading might add some weight to the occasion, but at a wedding people don't count on a Bible verse to see them through the day. At a church funeral, God is typically at the center of things. Even God's apparent silence at death can focus our attention, causing us to wonder and reflect. I always preferred a funeral because that's where the holy bits tended to be.

IN MY TRAVELS, I HAVE BEEN to some of the world's holiest places— not all of them, certainly, but enough of them—and by and large I found little that was holy about them. I remember visiting the grotto beneath the Church of the Nativity in Bethlehem, where according to tradition Jesus was born, and all I remember about it is the press of the crowds. I had to keep moving so that all of the pilgrims behind me could take their turn and see the place where Mary brought forth her firstborn child. I had pretty much the same reaction to the Church of the Holy Sepulchre in Jerusalem, St. Peter's Basilica in Rome, the Hagia Sophia in Istanbul, and even St. Peter's Cathedral in Geneva (John Calvin's church). I've seen all of them more than once, and I'm glad I did. But the unmistakable presence of God is not my lasting memory about any of them.

And yet, I think holiness can be connected to a place, even those I mentioned. For me the language of a "thin place" is often helpful. A "thin place" is where the membrane between this world and the next seems especially thin or porous, as though you could easily walk through and be in the presence of God. "Thin place," as I understand it, was originally a Celtic term, and for me it applies to the Isle of Iona, which lies off the western coast of Scotland. Something about the severe landscape and the ten-minute ferry ride from the Isle of

Mull to reach the place—as well as the abbey itself, which dates to 563 CE when St. Columba founded a monastic community there—give it an otherworldly feel, a place where God must be present, or at least available.

Mount Sinai, with St. Catherine's Monastery at its base, has been another of those places for me, a place where Christians have claimed, down through the centuries, to feel the unmistakable presence of God. I once climbed Mount Sinai with my nephew, arriving at the base of the mountain well after midnight, climbing through the night, and then once at the top waiting for the sun to rise over the Gulf of Aqaba. We could smell incense at dawn coming from an old Russian Orthodox Church, and in the early light we were surprised to find around us hundreds of other pilgrims from around the world who had also made the climb in darkness. It's hard to say exactly why these and not others are "thin places" for me, but I have a guess.

Annie Dillard has written in *Pilgrim at Tinker Creek* that there are two kinds of "seeing." One is the garden variety kind of seeing where you strain to pay attention to what's happening around you, as I always have in places like the Church of the Nativity. To see in this sense, you've got to work hard to quiet other voices within (and to block out the crowds of tourists). But there is another kind of seeing, according to Dillard, that involves "a letting go." You don't seek; instead, you wait. It isn't prayer, as she explains it; it's grace. The feeling comes to you, unexpectedly and mysteriously. You find yourself standing in a small chapel at the Sea of Galilee with church members you love, and you remember in that moment where you are and what you are doing. It's then that the place becomes holy.

TWENTY-SIX YEARS AFTER Sarah's baptism, she was ordained to the ministry of Word and Sacrament in the Presbyterian Church (USA), and once again I had a part in the service—not to throw water around this time, but to participate in the laying on of hands and to preach the sermon.

In my sermon that afternoon I mentioned Barbara Brown Taylor's book *An Altar in the World*, and I told the story from the book about Taylor's father teaching her to be observant of the world around her, what she learned to call the "practice of paying attention." For Taylor paying attention had become in her life and in her ministry a spiritual practice, right up there with prayer and Bible reading. But in Taylor's telling, the paying attention she has in mind is not straining; it is letting go. She would lie on the ground in the backyard, along with her father and younger sister, and while looking up into the night sky they would notice all sorts of things that you typically don't see unless you're paying attention: "All I remember is lying there beside [my father and sister] looking into a sky I had never really looked into before, or at least never for so long."

In my ordination sermon I told Sarah what I have come to see as true—namely, that to be a Minister of Word and Sacrament means to pay attention, to be observant, to find the holy, not only in the night sky (as Taylor has), but also in the everyday, in the committee meetings, and in the routine of ministry. I acknowledged that this, of course, is the work of every person of faith, but the Minister of Word and Sacrament, the steward of the mysteries of God, has the privilege and responsibility of devoting lots of time to it. The church members we serve, I said, will expect that we'll be able to do it, that in any old moment or setting, in a hospital room or next to the Sea of Galilee, we'll be able to talk about the divine presence and help others to see it too.

Leaders and Best, Champions of the West

I am grateful for all those dark years, even though in retrospect they seem like a long, bitter prayer that was answered finally.

Marilynne Robinson, *Gilead*

The search for truth takes you where the evidence leads you, even if, at first, you don't want to go there.

Bart D. Ehrman,
Forged: Writing in the Name of God

AT MY FIRST MEETING WITH THE ELDERS at the Ann Arbor church, the chair of the membership committee presented a list of one thousand names to erase from the inactive roll of the church. That came as a punch to the gut.

The second punch, almost a knockout, came a minute later when she presented a second motion to move more than five hundred names from the active roll to the inactive roll. No prayer was offered, no statements of regret and sadness were made, no one said much of anything. It was treated as a matter of business, requiring a motion, a second, and then a vote, yea or nay. The committee chair didn't think any of it was worth calling to my attention prior to the meeting. I was blindsided.

The church that had been presented to me, on its upbeat information form, as having 2,200 members, the largest in the presbytery, the flagship church, had become a 1,700-member church with two votes by the elders. The Ann Arbor church was now the same size as the church in Wheaton, the one I had just left behind, and not nearly as healthy.

I realize now that the blow I experienced was not to my gut, but to my ego. In my move from Wheaton to Ann Arbor, I thought I was trading up, going to a bigger church, achieving at long last what all my training had prepared me for. I had finally become the successful white male pastor in an expensive suit that I had admired all those years ago at seminary. But in a couple of votes on a Tuesday night, I realized that I had not achieved anything at all. In career terms I had made a lateral move. The deception eventually turned out to be a gift, but I didn't see it that way on that particular night—and not for several years afterward.

THE INACTIVE ROLL IS TYPICALLY a pastoral matter, as Presbyterians like to think about it. The idea is that the church spends two years trying to win back inactive members to the (active) life of the church. In reality, however, attempts to contact inactive members during that two-year period, especially on a scale as large as the Ann Arbor church faced, often amount to no more than a postcard asking if the member wishes to remain on the membership roll. No reply is usually the end of the matter. The name is then erased.

I had been in Ann Arbor less than a month before my first session meeting and had no more than an inkling that the church had been struggling. I knew, for example, that the interim pastor had been sick and had taken several weeks away from his work to recover from surgery, but I didn't know that in his absence some of the usual tasks of a church during an interim were neglected. Unpleasant but nevertheless important tasks, such as cleaning up the membership rolls. I had called a few people in presbytery leadership to ask about the church, but these people usually prefer to say nothing out of loyalty to the church and its search committee. I even called the previous pastor for his sense of where the church was. But getting answers about what is really happening within a church is notoriously difficult. I obviously didn't ask the right questions. In my defense I didn't know which questions to ask.

One evening, after my name had been released to the congregation as the search committee's candidate for the position of pastor, my wife, younger daughter, and I drove to Ann Arbor from Wheaton to participate in a get-acquainted meeting in the church's social hall. I would be invited to introduce myself, and members would be invited to ask me questions. As I was making my way from the car to the church, a man I did not recognize went by me in a kind of trot, as if late for the meeting. As he passed, he said, "It's not as bad as they told you!" I laughed, thinking it was a joke. As it turned out, it wasn't.

The man was chair of the church's personnel committee. He had a fine reputation in the community because he had recently (and successfully) argued a case before the US Supreme Court on behalf of the University of Michigan. I didn't know it then, just as I didn't know a lot of other things then, but the man would soon be moving out of the state to accept a new position, leaving behind a church staff that, let's say, had not received the attention it needed during the interim.

Also, in the category of important matters not disclosed, I learned soon after my arrival that the church faced a lawsuit stemming from an accident on a youth mission trip. A teenager fell from a roof and broke bones in her foot and ankle. The injury was serious, but not life-threatening. The parents, who were not church members, filed suit against the church and the youth leaders. By the time I arrived all of the youth leaders had been deposed and, in their telling, they had been made to look careless and negligent in their leadership roles. On the night before the trial was to begin, the youth leaders met with the trial lawyer and me in my office—to pray, to support each other, and to hear some last-minute assurance from the trial lawyer. The next day we learned that the lawsuit had been settled a few minutes before the trial began.

As I put all of this together, I began to recognize other issues. Some were small but telling. I noticed that no one thought to dust or clean the pastor's office after the interim had left. The bookshelves were covered with a thick layer of dust, as though they had not been touched in a long time. The carpet was dirty and had not been vacuumed. The windows, which looked out on a lovely lawn, were grimy. My first pastoral chore was to empty my waste basket. I looked around the church and began to see other signs of neglect. The building was old, but of greater concern was that it had not been well maintained. If you saw a person so obviously not taking care of himself, you might wonder about his self-image. Curiously, though, self-image was not a problem in Ann Arbor.

THE FIRST PRESBYTERIAN CHURCH OF ANN ARBOR is directly adjacent to the University of Michigan campus, at a remarkable location on Washtenaw Avenue, a well-known artery through the center of the city. Nearby there were many handsome sorority and fraternity houses. Parking, which had been a problem from my first day in Wheaton, was no problem for the Ann Arbor church. There was ample parking, so much in fact that the youth group earned a great deal of money each year for mission trips by charging visitors to park during the annual Ann Arbor Art Fair. The church had size, resources, location, and parking, everything a vibrant, thriving church could ask for. And at several points during its nearly two-hundred-year history, it had been a thriving church.

As with most Presbyterian churches with impressive appearances, the exterior of the church was featured on stationery, newspaper ads, and everywhere the church wanted to announce itself. I tried hard to understand this disconnect—a fine building, history, and location, but in many places worn, tired, and dirty. Church members didn't wonder how the church could be better, because to them it was already pretty good, better than most.

As a university town, one with a highly regarded undergraduate program and several highly ranked graduate schools, Ann Arbor attracts more than its share of very bright and talented people. There is an unmistakable academic energy in the air and an excitement about being the best. Even the university's famous fight song— "The Victors" —boasts of being "leaders and best" and "champions of the west." This ethos could be found everywhere in the city, even where it had not been earned.

My wife came to Ann Arbor with a JD from Rutgers University and an excellent resume in the private practice of law, but was told early on, rather colorfully, that her JD and law experience didn't count for much in Ann Arbor and that she would have a difficult time finding a job—a prediction that turned out to be correct. A young woman who was a member of the church and who worked at the University of Michigan Hospital once told me without a trace of humor that her MD, which came from a highly regarded medical school in another state, might as well have been from a nonaccredited school.

Still, I was excited. I imagined that I would grow and thrive and perhaps have more time to write than I had in Wheaton. The move to Ann Arbor was everything I had dreamed about. I thought it would be my last church before retirement. It was big and important, just as I had hoped, and it was in my home state. I was home at last.

AS TIME PASSED, THOUGH, Ann Arbor began to feel less like home. I began to see the "leaders and best" and "champions of the west" phenomenon everywhere I looked, including the obituaries in the *Ann Arbor News*. I had never seen an obituary that covered not one, but several newspaper columns, reading much like someone's curriculum vitae, with every degree, professional association, and publication listed. This practice was in sharp contrast to the midwestern modesty I had grown up with. I remembered my father-in-law's obituary from a few years earlier and its single-sentence description of his life— "servant of Jesus Christ." His children didn't think to mention his dental degree from the University of Michigan or his service in World War II or his Distinguished Alumni Award from the college he attended. In Ann Arbor there was competition to be the best even in death.

In a sermon about the importance of Christian baptism, I told a story about removing my diplomas from my office wall and storing them in my closet. The decision, I said, was a recognition in my own life that my baptism was the only credential that really mattered. At the door after worship, a man approached me as I was shaking hands, and in a louder-than-necessary voice he let me know how hard he had worked on his own degrees and how his diplomas were going to remain on his office walls, thank you very much. I knew I had touched a nerve.

Another time, on a tour of Israel with church members, a guide had just finished a brief talk on the mosaics at the Church of the Primacy of Saint Peter near the Sea of Galilee, when a member of my group spoke up to correct him. All tour groups in Israel are assigned a guide; it's required by the government. And all guides in my experience are very well-trained for their work. However, they are typically not university faculty with graduate degrees, say, in art history. So, the church member, a university faculty member, gave a second lecture to our group about the mosaics and refuted much of what we had been told. It was a humiliating moment for our guide, and it showed in his facial expression and in his demeanor for the rest of the tour.

If I had known about the tour group member's expertise in ancient mosaics, I would have passed this information along to our guide. But I didn't, and this unfortunate incident was the result.

I'M STILL NOT SURE WHAT TO SAY about the church staff, even after all these years, though it was the most difficult issue I faced at the Ann Arbor church. I suppose I had been spoiled by the people I had worked with previously. Even where I struggled with a few relationships, I never doubted their dedication to the work or their desire to get along with their colleagues.

From my first staff meeting at the church in Ann Arbor, I was aware of an unhealthy atmosphere. I had heard stories about shouting matches at staff meetings, with staff members storming out and slamming the door, but in the first few weekly meetings the staff was on its best behavior. It was not to last.

I was frequently at a loss about what to do. I had never witnessed certain behaviors—one staff member insulting another at a staff meeting, for example. My clearest (and least satisfying) memory of my years at the Ann Arbor church is of replacing staff members, one by one. But even the addition of bright, talented, and eager staff members seemed to do little to change an entrenched staff culture. A fine new campus pastor, with a refreshing presence in worship and terrific insights about how to recharge our campus ministry, left sooner than I would have liked. He found the staff environment toxic, and he left.

But there were also happy exceptions. David Krehbiel, a retired pastor who worked a few days each week for the church by calling on sick and homebound members, left his resignation letter on my desk so that it was the first thing I saw as I unpacked my boxes. David had an old-school view of church staffs. His thinking was that everyone on the church staff should submit a resignation when a new pastor arrived, allowing the new person to form a new team. I went to see David immediately and asked him to stay, which he agreed to do, but the catch was that he wanted to help me find his successor, which he did.

On David's last Sunday, he gave a children's sermon that was one of the most memorable I have ever heard (and I have heard many memorable children's sermons). The theme of the sermon was "Who will replace us?" He explained to the children that he was retiring, but he then pointed at me and a few others at the front of the church who, he said, would one day be retiring too. So, the question for the children was, "Who will replace us?" It was one of the most touching and heartfelt approaches I have ever heard to the issue of asking young people—*very* young people, in this case—to consider a life of ministry.

The person David identified as his choice for replacing him was Melissa Anne Rogers. She was my choice too, but David's endorsement turned out to be critically important. Not only was Melissa Anne ordained, but she had completed coursework toward a PhD in psychology and had an extraordinary gift for understanding and working with church members.

Once, a young woman from the congregation died unexpectedly, and her young children discovered her body slumped over her laundry basket in the basement of their home. The entire church was devasted. There was a great deal to do, and the situation required a fair amount of skill, what has rightly been called "pastoral imagination." The school where the young woman's children attended decided to cancel classes the morning of the funeral service so that everyone, students and faculty, could attend. I had officiated at many funerals over the years, but I had never faced a congregation filled with children.

Melissa Anne didn't hesitate. She said, "I'll do a children's sermon." I was skeptical but had no better idea. I trusted her instincts.

During the funeral Melissa Anne invited all of the children in the church to come forward and stand with her around the communion table. A few dozen accepted the invitation. Melissa Anne may have knelt to speak to them at eye level, but what I remember is that she spoke to them in plain but not condescending language about what had happened, and how sad it was, and how our faith could make sense of the worst situations in life. Melissa Anne was wonderful that day. She was so good that, when she was finished, I realized there was no need for me to climb into the pulpit and preach the sermon I had prepared. She said everything that needed to be said that day, and she said it so that eight-, nine-, and ten-year-old children could understand.

IN SPITE OF THE STRUGGLES I experienced in Ann Arbor, I have fond memories that go a long way toward redeeming the experience.

One of them was Robben Fleming, who had been president of the University of Michigan from 1968 to 1979, one of the most difficult periods in American history for colleges and universities. Fleming came to Michigan from the University of Wisconsin–Madison where he went to law school, taught, and later become chancellor. He also worked as a lawyer in the US Army during World War II, had experience as a labor negotiator, and was once president of the Corporation for Public Broadcasting. His skills at dealing with campus unrest at the University of Wisconsin made him an attractive candidate at Michigan, which was just beginning to experience serious turmoil.

Fleming was in his nineties when I came to know him, and he was living then at an assisted-living facility in Ann Arbor. But he was sharp mentally and still very much enjoyed the church's monthly men's luncheon. I offered to give him a ride each month, and our time together in the car involved some of the best stories about his experiences that I have ever heard.

One of my favorites involved the desire of students who were anti-Vietnam War activists to dig a symbolic bomb crater in the Diag, the heart of the central campus. Fleming, who was justifiably proud of his negotiating skills, somehow convinced the students that they had a terrific idea, but that they should dig the crater elsewhere, due to the possibility of underground cables in the Diag. In Fleming's telling of the story, the students accepted his reasons and began to dig at the alternate location, only to quit after a few hours because the work was hard. I remember that at this point Fleming laughed with great satisfaction at the story. He gave the students what they wanted and had somehow managed to preserve the center of the campus. It was my honor to officiate at his funeral.

Another fond memory was being around for my younger daughter's undergraduate years. She didn't live at home, but I would see her often, usually crossing campus on her bicycle. We would also meet for lunch each week at a restaurant of her choice. Because of my daughter (and tickets she secured because of her student status), I was able to go with her to lectures by General David Petraeus and the poet Maya Angelou, among others. I was able to see former vice president Al Gore present his slideshow known as *An Inconvenient Truth*, which later became a film and won two Academy Awards. My daughter and I even saw two plays by the Royal Shakespeare Company during its residency in Ann Arbor.

Not exactly a fond memory, but certainly a vivid one, the Ann Arbor church was the site of a demonstration one Sunday morning by members of the Westboro Baptist Church, founded by Fred Phelps in Topeka, Kansas. The members of the Westboro Church were in Ann Arbor to protest a movie, shown on campus the previous evening, about a young gay man named Matthew Shepard who was brutally beaten, tortured, and tied to a barbed wire fence outside Laramie, Wyoming. As the largest church on one of the most visible streets in Ann Arbor, the First Presbyterian Church was a natural protest site before the group left town the next morning. Signs carried in front of our church included "God Hates Fags," "Thank God for Dead Soldiers," and "Sin and Shame, not Pride."

My first inclination was to bring hot chocolate and donuts to the protesters as an expression of welcome and hospitality, but the police convinced me that these were professional demonstrators and that I should simply allow them to do what they came to do. In an announcement the previous week, I encouraged members of the church to be kind, engage the protesters in civil conversation, and invite them in for worship. The Westboro Baptist people, as it turned out, were not interested in having conversations or in attending our morning worship. Still, it was one of the most interesting Sunday mornings of my career, and the congregation that morning was unusually large. I think that getting up and coming to church that day was a silent but effective counterprotest. And for one morning I was proud to be their pastor.

AFTER FIVE YEARS IN ANN ARBOR, the First Presbyterian Church of Fort Lauderdale unexpectedly made contact with me and asked if I would be interested in becoming their pastor. I was ready to say yes.

God Loves All Kinds of People

Every once in a while, life can be eloquent.

Frederick Buechner, *A Room Called Remember*

It all means more than I can tell you. So you must not judge what I know by what I find words for.

Marilynne Robinson, *Gilead*

WHAT I WOULD PREFER TO REMEMBER about my years in Fort Lauderdale are the fishing trips to the Everglades I took with a member of the church there, Birch Wiley, who was not born in Florida, but who lived much of his life there—in other words, more of a native than most of the people who live in Florida these days.

Birch would pick me up in the early morning darkness, we would stop at McDonald's for a breakfast sandwich (his idea, not mine), and then we would head out for miles on I-75, or Alligator Alley, which connects the east and west sides of the state. I forget where we turned off each time, but Birch was always able to find the turnoff, even in the dark. He drove a few miles more after getting off the interstate, and then we stopped to put his decrepit fishing boat into one of the canals. We never saw another human being, but the canals were often lined with alligators, thousands of them, sunning themselves and keeping an eye on us as we motored along. One time, when I reached toward shore to grab a tangled line, Birch grabbed my arm and pointed to a gator who was silently watching from a few feet away. I probably still have my right arm today because Birch thought it better to cut the line than to retrieve the tangled one.

We would fish for hours, through some of the hottest hours of day, and then finally we would head back to the boat launch, clean our fish, and set out for home. I should mention that Birch was the one who scaled and filleted the few largemouth bass we caught, while I watched and admired his handiwork. I never asked if I could take a turn. We would have been there all night, as I think he knew. As it was, we never got back to Fort Lauderdale until dinner time, and I was always glad to get home, take a shower, have dinner, and go to bed. Those were some of the best days off I've ever had.

I mention Birch at this point because our hours together—sometimes talking, sometimes with him teaching me how to use a casting rod, and sometimes sitting silently with fishing lines in the water—are reminders of what I loved most about being a pastor. I enjoyed being with people like Birch, I loved hearing his stories, and I learned a great deal from him about the church in Fort Lauderdale and its history by listening to him talk about it. I also learned a great deal about the history of the Everglades from Birch, and I have no reason to doubt the story he told. He loved the area and was heartbroken by the ways it was slowly being changed and degraded, often because of misguided efforts to make it better. Ironically, the canals where we fished did as much as anything to ruin the delicate ecosystem. As I think back to the churches I have served, it's people like Birch who make me glad that I was a pastor.

Birch, of course, was not the only interesting person at the Fort Lauderdale church. South Florida was so different from anywhere else I have lived that I found the people endlessly interesting. Fort Lauderdale, especially the part of it where the church was located, has a great deal of wealth, or else (it wasn't always clear) people pretended to have a great deal of wealth. Either way, many of them drove luxury cars and lived in gorgeous homes along the many canals. Some people stayed behind their gated entrances, but others, like Birch, were more a part of the community, visible in stores and restaurants and community events.

My theory about ministry was that if I could build enough relationships with church members, like the one I had with Birch, then I could address difficult subjects when I needed to—and expect to be heard when I did so. Those relationships, so my thinking went, would allow me to say what I wanted to say, what I was often too reluctant to say. I was trained to think of this as being prophetic, saying what people didn't want to hear.

In my years in Wheaton, I banked a considerable amount of trust, but then ended up never using it for social justice issues. I nudged the church in the direction of mission, it is true, and I'm proud of the work we did, but this was a direction that members already wanted to go. Getting them moving didn't require much effort. I wish I had used their trust for more.

I now see, though, that my theory was wrong—being prophetic doesn't have to wait for trust or whatever I thought I needed. I think I was utterly wrong about what it means to be prophetic. The prophets of the Old Testament didn't wait until they were sure that people would listen before they spoke. They spoke because they couldn't keep quiet. They spoke because they were convinced that what they had to say was true. So their authority was rooted not in relationships, but in truth, in the words God put in their mouths. What they said was true, and those who heard it could accept it or reject it, but that didn't change the truth of it.

IN FORT LAUDERDALE, I WAS AWARE THAT I had an opportunity to speak truth to the large gay and lesbian population in Fort Lauderdale. More important, I had an opportunity to speak truth *to my congregation* about the large gay and lesbian population in Fort Lauderdale. It would have been a prophetic word, too, and probably not a welcome word to most. It would have been a word, moreover, not heard in many churches in Fort Lauderdale, which would have made the word all the more important. I knew there were gay and lesbian people not just in the surrounding neighborhoods, but in my church, who longed to be seen and heard and welcomed.

One of them was my high school guidance counselor who had retired to south Florida with his partner of more than fifty years. As a high school student, I did not know about his sexual orientation, and when I met him again after all those years, I realized that he had kept both his identity and the most important relationship of his life a secret from the Christian schools in which he taught. But there he was each Sunday, with his partner, always in the same pew, singing and praying and worshiping with everyone else.

In addition to my high school guidance counselor, I knew there were gay and lesbian members of the choir. One of them was a tenor who was always everyone's choice to sing at the funeral of a loved one. I suppose most people knew his sexual orientation, but it was something no one talked about. He was expected not to talk about it too. In the silence, some people felt pretty good about their acceptance and welcome. What would not have been welcome, however, was any kind of official acceptance and welcome.

Into this situation, and into this community, I spoke no prophetic words. I let some people down, and I regret it still.

One time I preached a sermon based on Acts 10, the story of Peter seeing a vision and being directed to "kill and eat" the unclean animals that were displayed for him on "something like a large sheet coming down, being lowered to the ground by its four corners" (Acts 10:11). I forget now what I said in the sermon, though it might have been, "God sure can be surprising!"

After the sermon, a church member and a member of the search committee came to the door where I was shaking hands and said, "Doug, I'm so relieved. I've heard sermons based on that text about how supposedly God loves all kinds of people, you know, including gay and lesbian people. I was so worried that you were going to go there."

I remember those words now because they stung then just as they sting today. But I told myself, as I always did, that the church had bigger concerns. First, though, one more story.

THE LOW POINT IN MY RELATIONSHIP with the Presbyterian Church came in May 2012, when the Presbytery of Tropical Florida, the presbytery of which I was a member, voted to dismiss nine congregations.

"Dismissal" is a term in church law that refers to the way congregations are allowed to leave. A church can't just decide one day to leave the Presbyterian Church. A church must be dismissed to another body, a denomination, which agrees to accept that church. And the dismissed church can't just leave with its building, parking lot, endowment, and any other assets, because all of that, its property, belongs to the presbytery.

This legal matter has been tested in the courts, and each time the presbytery has prevailed. Congregations can leave if they want to, but they must leave without their property. To leave *and* take property requires a considerable amount of wrangling, which is what happened in the Presbytery of Tropical Florida during my first years there. The churches that wanted to leave already knew the rules, so what was left was to negotiate the separation agreement, what came to be known, rather optimistically, as "gracious separation." For a couple of years, every meeting, every decision, and every conversation were consumed by this wrangling—how nine unhappy congregations would eventually be allowed to leave because they couldn't stand one more minute with the rest of us.

The process has been likened to the end of a marriage because that's what it feels like, except in this case, on this particular day in May, there were nine divorces. There would have been others, but those others, for various reasons, hadn't completed the complicated process.

I have never enjoyed presbytery meetings and have never looked forward to attending them, but I always went because I learned early on that that's what you do if you are a Presbyterian pastor. I am a member of the presbytery. The presbytery holds my credentials for ministry. The other pastors are my colleagues, and I am accountable to them, just as they are to me. It is a relationship, a covenant, that I have honored for more than forty years. But I have never attended a more dispiriting meeting than this one.

The nine churches that left were among the largest in the presbytery. Their departure represented a loss of nearly a third of the overall membership, 3,800 members out of 13,525. If the dismissals had happened all at once, in a single vote, the day might have been better,

maybe even tolerable, but the Presbyterian Church is known for doing things decently and in order, and the decent and orderly thing to
do in this case was to handle each one individually—a process that
consumed the better part of a day.

One by one, representatives from the nine churches that wanted
out would stand and give a summary of their reasons. They hadn't
changed, they said, as if reading from the same script, but the denomination had changed. It had moved away from them. It no longer recognized the authority of scripture. It had embraced universalism. And
the last straw, in 2011, it had passed Amendment 10A, which deleted
the so-called "fidelity-chastity" requirement for ordination from the
Form of Government, meaning that ordination would henceforth be
open to gays and lesbians. After the motion was made, seconded, and
passed, each of the nine groups hugged each other and celebrated.
The burden of being connected to the rest of us was over. They were
free at last, thank God almighty, free at last.

By the end of the day, I was spent. I had no enthusiasm for those
who had left or for those who had stayed. I was nearly sixty years old
and had, at that point, given thirty-five years of my life to the Presbyterian Church, and I had fallen out of love with it. I had quit going to
meetings of the General Assembly years earlier for pretty much the
same reason—talking and fighting about the same issues over and
over. I tried talking to other pastors about it, but I found that, by and
large, they were glad it was over. They felt relieved. The decision had
been made, and now, as far as they were concerned, the matter was
over. We could finally get on, they said, with being the church. No
more fighting—or at least no more fighting over this issue.

I wanted to feel as sanguine about it as they did but couldn't. Besides, I had a few other things to think about.

MY YEARS AT THE ANN ARBOR CHURCH began with a series of
unpleasant surprises, mostly in the form of undisclosed problems. My
years at the Fort Lauderdale church began in the form of too much
disclosure. I knew before I accepted the call what my work would be

and decided, when I accepted the call, to devote my remaining years of ministry to doing this work.

Two issues were going to need all of my experience and ability as a pastor.

First, my predecessor abruptly resigned from the church and renounced his ordination in the days leading up to Easter 2007, telling a reporter from the *Sun Sentinel*, the Fort Lauderdale newspaper, that his decision was the result of "extreme personal, physical and emotional stress in my life."

What the *Sun Sentinel* did not report was that a woman had created a website that she filled with sexually charged and embarrassing emails, text messages, and voice mails, all from my predecessor, all addressed to her. Someone—it's not clear who did this—placed the website address under the windshield wiper of every car in the church parking lot one Sunday morning during worship.

So "extreme personal, physical, and emotional stress"? I can understand why.

My predecessor sent the news of his resignation to the congregation in a letter that went to all 2,800 members. According to the *Sun Sentinel*, in front-page coverage of the situation, my predecessor's "action leaves the top spot vacant at the largest South Florida congregation in the Presbyterian Church (USA). Founded in 1912, First Presbyterian is a church home to many of the city's business, political and community leaders, including Miami Dolphins owner H. Wayne Huizenga and Fort Lauderdale Mayor Jim Naugle."

The resignation had many consequences for the church, among them the loss of nearly 1,000 members and $1 million from the annual operating budget, all occurring within a year of the resignation. Instead of making cuts to the budget, laying off staff, or reducing salaries, the church drew heavily from its endowments during the interim in an attempt to keep going as before.

No one on the search committee attempted to hide or minimize the situation. The matter was public, of course, but to their credit they were open about what had happened and what needed to be done.

They freely expressed their disappointment with my predecessor and their grief over what had happened to their church. No one offered a defense for my predecessor's behavior; mostly what I heard was a great sadness that a singular talent had been wasted. "He had a problem with the broads" was how one older woman in the congregation sadly described the matter to me. A few other comments were just as colorful.

The search committee's interest in me seemed clear and may even have been made explicit. They hoped I would be the experienced senior pastor who would lead the church, both its members and its staff, beyond this unfortunate episode.

Second, under my predecessor's leadership, the church initiated a $22 million building campaign, with more than two-thirds of the money either pledged or already given. The plan was to develop a property owned by the church along Las Olas Boulevard, one of the premier shopping and dining streets in the United States, similar to Worth Avenue in Palm Beach or Rodeo Drive in Beverly Hills. The new building would feature a large multipurpose room or gymnasium, a parking garage, and retail shops on the first floor along Las Olas. The latter was not the church's idea, but it was a compromise with the zoning board to get approval for the project. I suspect the city wasn't happy about losing so much tax revenue to a tax-exempt organization. Parking on Sundays would be free for those attending worship, but parking during the week would generate revenue for the church and its mission. It was a plan of ambitious proportions.

Curiously, during breaks in my longest interview with the search committee, members confided to me their doubts about the plan, even though publicly they endorsed what the church and its leadership wanted to do. One member of the committee whispered to me during a break that "the building is unnecessary, especially in our current circumstances," but he acknowledged that I would be under enormous pressure to get the building built. "Not a good position to be in," he said.

Prior to my arrival, under pressure from the neighborhood over the scale of the building, the church had downsized the project considerably, reducing the height of the building and creating more open space. The projected cost of the revised plan was around $16 million, still a considerable challenge for the church.

If the neighbors were pleased with the downsizing, it wasn't evident from their behavior. The church was being cast in an increasingly negative light in the local newspaper. What most people knew about the church was that it was in conflict with its neighbors. The neighborhood surrounding the church consisted of large and expensive homes, some of them directly on the New River, which flows from the Everglades to the Atlantic Ocean. The closer to the ocean, the more expensive the homes, and the church was a little over two miles from the beach. The church, as the neighbors saw it, would bring too much traffic to a peaceful, quiet, and exclusive neighborhood.

Initially, the church's attitude to the neighbors was combative, and the strategy was to overwhelm them with numbers at meetings of the city's planning and zoning board. The church also hired three registered lobbyists, whose job was to meet with the mayor, city commissioners, and local neighborhood associations to win support for the project. The cost of the lobbying effort came from money already given to the building campaign and amounted to more than $100,000.

On one of my first days in the church office, I asked the chair of the building campaign what the vision was, why it was so important to keep pushing ahead in the face of so much opposition. He paused and then pointed to boxes of files about the project. "It's all in there," he said.

The truth is, no one seemed to know what the new building was for, except to provide space for the church's inevitable growth. The land was there, it had to be developed, and the plan was in place to develop it. What more was there to say? Some members were pleased that questions were being asked about the wisdom of proceeding and asked for their money back. Others cancelled their pledges. Church leaders decided to return any contributions to the building campaign, but they were determined to keep going.

After the church won approval from the city to start the project, I found a fundraising professional in the congregation who explained to the leaders what a successful campaign looked like. Ours did not look anything like a successful campaign. She explained our situation with a persuasive PowerPoint presentation and noted that many members still very much liked the idea of building, but *only* if someone else paid for it. In a painful vote, the elders decided in February 2013 to abandon the plan. After the vote the campaign chair left the meeting and the church.

ONE MONTH LATER I WAS CONTACTED by the International Protestant Church of Zürich. The search committee wondered if I would be willing to be considered for their vacant senior pastor position. I had intended to remain in Florida for the rest of my career, but my work, it seemed to me, was finished. And the thought of leaving the Presbyterian Church behind was appealing. I agreed to interview.

Ich bin ein Züricher

You are God's tool. He wills to wear you out by use, not by idleness. Oh, happy man, whom he calls to His work!

The Latin Works and the Correspondence
of Huldreich Zwingli, vol. 2

Never knew before what eternity was made for. It is to give some of us a chance to learn German.

Mark Twain, *Notebook 14*,
November 1877–July 1878

Over the years, whenever someone asked what I did for a living, I was always careful to say that I was a *Presbyterian* pastor, making clear that I was different from those other pastors—Methodists, Baptists, Pentecostals, and worse. I now realize that this careful distinction was lost on most people.

Few people today know (or care) what a Presbyterian is or how a Presbyterian pastor differs from others. I seem to be one of the few people who knows that the only active clergyman to sign the Declaration of Independence was a Presbyterian (John Witherspoon), but if I were to offer up this bit of trivia to someone—to the person sitting next to me on an airplane, let's say—the response would be a puzzled look, as if to say, "Why does that matter?" The answer is that it once mattered to me, but it matters now to a vanishingly few other people.

To me, the label "Presbyterian pastor" meant, first of all, that I went to school: I completed an undergraduate degree and then three additional years at an accredited theological institution, where I was awarded the MDiv degree. Not only that, but I was required to gain a reading knowledge of ancient Hebrew and New Testament Greek. (Presbyterians are one of the few church groups left to insist that their pastors have at least some exposure to the biblical languages.) To be ordained as a Presbyterian, I was required to pass some rigorous ordination exams, including one in biblical content, another in biblical exegesis (making use of those biblical languages), and a handful of others. To be a Presbyterian pastor also meant that I have been given a thorough psychological evaluation and screening, which included two and a half days of testing and a lengthy meeting with a psychiatrist (somehow a few bad apples still manage to sneak through). To me, all of this meant something, and to a certain extent (more than I realize), it still does.

Always, though, as I think about my pedigree, I am reminded of how the apostle Paul described his own pedigree in his letter to the Philippians: "circumcised on the eighth day, a member of the people of Israel, of the tribe of Benjamin, a Hebrew born of Hebrews; as to the law, a Pharisee; as to zeal, a persecutor of the church; as to righteousness under the law, blameless."

So, in his first-century context, his pedigree was pretty good (better than most), which makes his assessment all the more startling: "I regard [all of that] as rubbish." I once learned in a New Testament exegesis class that the word often translated as "rubbish" means something far more earthy. But there it is: the central author of the New Testament takes a dim view of pedigrees, or at least finds them worth nothing compared to "knowing Christ Jesus my Lord."

WHEN I MOVED TO SWITZERLAND in January 2014 to become pastor of the International Protestant Church of Zürich, I maintained my membership in the Presbyterian Church (USA) and continued to pay my pension dues. I was even required to get permission to "labor outside the bounds" of my presbytery. I surrendered much of my identity as a *Presbyterian* pastor to take the new position, but I had been so thoroughly absorbed into a particular identity that I continued to think of myself as a Presbyterian. Even though I had fallen out of love with the PCUSA, I couldn't imagine severing my ties to it.

IPC, as it is known, is unaffiliated with any denominational entity. It belongs to a network of other international churches in Europe and the Middle East (the AICEME), but that network exists primarily as a friendship and support group for the pastors of those churches. IPC also has a "covenant" relationship with the state church—or *Landeskirche*—which allowed it to offer employment contracts to pastors from outside Switzerland who were, like me, native English speakers.

So, for the first time in my career, I was on my own, and my church was on its own. Like many nondenominational churches in the United States, IPC was free to develop its own constitution and by-laws, as well as all of its own norms and traditions, which felt entirely normal to some members, but not to others. IPC was also free to call pastors from any denomination or country or theological tradition it wanted. The constitution specified that candidates for pastor should have a theological degree, but the precise meaning of this language was vague. Did that mean a degree from a two-year Bible college? Or did that mean something more? No one seemed to know.

I discovered early on that no one at IPC knew what my Presbyterian identity meant. One or two members from the United Kingdom, maybe, but no one else. Most people at IPC were from various churches around the world—India, Pakistan, South Korea, Taiwan, Hong Kong, Japan, Malaysia, the Philippines, Australia, Ethiopia, Nigeria, Ghana, South Africa, Lesotho, Lebanon, Peru, Brazil, the United Kingdom, Germany, the Netherlands, Switzerland, Norway, Poland, the United States, and more. More than two dozen nationalities and language groups were present on any given Sunday morning. I must say, it was overwhelming, especially at the beginning. Our only common denominator, beyond Christian faith, was that we all spoke English, some better than others. No one seemed to care where I had gone to school or what I had studied or how many seminary presidents I knew personally. No one cared about my training in the biblical languages or my rigorous ordination exams. No one I met had ever heard of putting a pastor through a psychological evaluation; a clear call from God, along with a compelling call story, was all anybody seemed to care about.

In a way, this was a refreshing change, a change I had been seeking for some time—to do ministry, to be a pastor, in a setting where denominational history and culture were unimportant, where status, wealth, and privilege counted as "rubbish." Happily, I seemed to find what I was looking for more than 4,000 miles from the United

States. IPC owned no buildings and had no endowment. The congregation rented space for morning worship from one church (the *Eglise réformée française*) and for evening worship from yet another church on the same street. Our office space was a few steps from both churches in an office building. Our Sunday school and youth group were also held in rented space—at the *Kantonsschule Stadelhofen*, a nearby high school.

Suddenly, after spending so much of my career maintaining, renovating, and occasionally expanding buildings, my church was a renter, subject to the whims of not one but multiple landlords. When morning worship at the French Reformed Church ran late, for example, our own morning worship started late. Members would mill around in front of the church until they were allowed in. I don't remember that anyone ever complained about this, but we were always aware that the space was not ours. We shared in the Christmas decorations, but had no role in planning them. We used the seating arrangement of the other congregation and were not free to experiment with our own. We could decorate a space for special worship services, but whatever we created had to be set up in the few minutes before our service began (and taken down a few minutes after it ended).

Some members used the language of "sojourner" to refer to our status, but the church never reflected much on what this might mean. A sojourner is a term used primarily in the Hebrew Bible to refer to a person or a group of people who are living temporarily in a place and must thereby rely on the goodwill of the people who live there, the hosts. Other translations of the Hebrew word include "resident alien" and "stranger." Frequently, the word is used as a reminder to treat others well because "you were once a sojourner too." I'm not sure where further reflection on the word would have taken us in our understanding of ourselves, though most members were themselves sojourners, living far from home, without a clear sense of belonging. It's possible that exploring all of this would have led to a deeper understanding of our identity, but mostly we were aware that as a church our existence was precarious, that we might one day be asked to move.

THE CHURCH I CAME TO IN ZÜRICH had just been through a "difficult season of ministry" (that artful expression again). There had been division, sides were taken, tempers in some cases were short, several people left to find another church, attendance was down, the budget showed a deficit, and the previous pastor's contract was not renewed. In other words, a situation similar to what I had found in one or two other churches I had served.

What I found, though, was that without a support structure, without any accountability, without a reliable lifeline, churches like IPC can (and often do) find themselves in serious trouble. A complaint to the presbytery about the personal behavior of a Presbyterian pastor usually triggers a response, perhaps an investigation, sometimes a censure, and in rare circumstances a removal. Presbyteries even have the authority to dismiss dysfunctional governing boards and to install, temporarily at least, a board made up of pastors and elders from the presbytery. Some of these support, accountability, and oversight mechanisms would undoubtedly have been beneficial to IPC. But accountability to and among other congregations wasn't the only feature of the Presbyterian Church I missed.

A church like IPC, which called itself into existence a few decades ago, has no creed, confession, or statement of faith. On the one hand, this was seen by some members as a strength. One former pastor was often quoted with admiration as having said, "We believe that Jesus Christ is Lord and that the Bible is God's word. Beyond that, we smile a lot." In practice, though, the lack of a statement of faith made church life far more complicated. Even reciting the Apostles' Creed in worship from time to time raised questions for some. I discovered the rub in several areas of church life, but almost immediately in the sacrament of baptism. I had been steeped in Reformed theology and was accustomed to baptizing babies. Many global Christians, I learned, subscribe to the notion of a believer's baptism and find the practice of infant baptism unfathomable.

For much of my career, if a theological conflict arose, I could point to the Presbyterian *Book of Confessions* and say, "That's what we believe," smiling, maybe even shrugging a little, as if to say, "I can't do anything about it." And so, the matter, whatever it was, would be resolved. At IPC, however, I found myself listening and accommodating more. My position on anything was never more than my position—interesting, sometimes infuriating, but never the final word. I was allowed to argue for my position, but I was expected to listen attentively to other positions, which I gladly did.

Several times during my years in Zürich I waded into Lake Zürich with a new believer and raised that person, sputtering for air, from the icy waters of death to resurrection life. I'm grateful to have had the opportunity to participate in a believer's baptism. I remember each one with fondness and gratitude. I have a special memory of a young woman from Africa (via Spain) named Nadia Ussene who came out of the water waving her arms and shouting. Her joy was so obvious and contagious that soon all of us, including all of the church members on shore, were doing the same thing. I realized with some sadness that Presbyterians seldom express their joy as spontaneously as Nadia did.

Out in the water, though, I would also think about my grandfather, the one I never met but who, according to my mother, would have been "so proud" to know that his grandson had become a pastor. Would he have been proud of my occasional departures from sound Reformed theology? What would he have made of the shouting and leaping for joy after a baptism? I'll never know, of course, but if he had become a pastor, as he had always wanted, I would like to think that he, too, would have waded out into the water and helped to raise a young woman to new life.

I never let go of the desire to gather members together and hammer out, once and for all, a statement of faith, but in the end I had to leave the task to my successor. I came away from my experience grateful for having within myself a theological center, not the answer to every question, but a set of core beliefs. I always knew who I was. I always knew, more or less, what I believed. I could listen, I could accommodate to some other points of view, and at times I could see the difference between the essentials and the nonessentials of the faith. Stripped of the need for prestige and power and wealth, I came to see the faith I learned in childhood for the wonderful gift it was.

IRONICALLY, GIVEN THE DECIDEDLY EVANGELICAL THEOLOGY of most members—and most global Christians, it seems—the most successful pastors at IPC over the years came from the liberal, mainline Presbyterian Church (USA). My predecessor, who was from Brazil and who was not Presbyterian, probably fit the evangelical ethos of IPC far better than I did, but where I was curious and willing to listen, he was certain about his beliefs and, I was told by some, could be authoritarian and argumentative. I can be authoritarian and argumentative, too, let's be honest, but something about my Presbyterian training made me welcoming and ecumenical, willing to look at all sides of an issue. I attended seminary classes with students from the entire range of the theological spectrum. Rather than dismissing other points of view, I (and my Presbyterian predecessors at IPC) wanted to understand, engage, and find areas of agreement.

Presbyterians can, in some circles, appear to be spineless and unwilling to take a strong stand on anything (the source of many old and uncomfortable jokes), but remarkably enough this trait has often made Presbyterians effective in an ecumenical setting and, as I discovered, in an international setting. I was always curious, always looking into theological matters that I didn't understand.

One night at dinner, at the home of a couple from India, I asked how they had met, thinking the question was an easy one, as it might be in the United States. I imagined that our new friends met while they were university students, dated for a while, and then married, because that described my own experience. Don't we often universalize from what we know? And so, I was astonished when the couple explained, hesitantly at first, that theirs was an arranged marriage. Even though the two had lived, studied, and worked abroad, they returned home one day to find that their parents had found them a spouse. They emphasized that their parents were not heavy-handed about it, that there was some room (not much) for negotiation, but that in the end they accepted their parents' decision.

My wife and I were worried at this point that we had intruded, that we had asked about something that was none of our business, so the couple from India quickly explained that the custom of arranged marriages, so deeply ingrained in their own culture, would probably come to an end with their family. Their boys were growing up in Switzerland, after all, and they knew nothing of these expectations. Their boys spoke Swiss German, had Swiss passports, and thought of themselves as Swiss. They would be eager to rid themselves of some old and hidebound customs.

Another couple we met would, in any other setting, have been described as a "mixed marriage": he was Swiss, and she was Thai. They had met at a bank in Chicago where both were working. She was his immediate supervisor. The husband's story, which he has undoubtedly told many times, was that his mother sternly warned him that when choosing a mate there were to be "no Germans and no Catholics." Disapproval for Germans and Catholics in Zürich, for a woman of her generation, would not have been unusual, which makes the punchline to the story all the more enjoyable. Before bringing his fiancée home to Switzerland to meet his mother, my friend Jürg wrote to his mother, "What about a Thai Buddhist?" That Thai woman, my dear friend Pia, converted to the Christian faith not long after they were married.

GLOBAL CHRISTIANS WERE NOT, IN MY EXPERIENCE, open to the idea of women as pastors. When our associate pastor left to become a pastor in the *Landeskirche*, a search committee was formed to find a new associate. At one of our early meetings, the chair of the committee suggested that we ask each person around the table for "deal breakers"—in other words, qualities and characteristics in a new pastor we would find unacceptable. It was clear to me that the chair and another member of the committee were worried that a woman might emerge as one of the finalists for the position, since several women had submitted applications.

I suggested in response that we do something different, that each committee member be given the opportunity to suggest qualities and characteristics that would be most desirable in the new pastor, a more positive approach. I realized that I had been outmaneuvered, however, and my suggestion received no traction. We listened to each other's deal breakers, and in the end the search committee voted not to look any further at the women who had applied. I was heartbroken about this and said so. My own daughter, I mentioned, would not be considered suitable for the church where I served as pastor. My concerns were noted but swept aside, and a few months later the committee recommended to the congregation a fine white, heterosexual male from the United States for the position. I had a high regard for the person who became our candidate—and still do—but the process troubled me. And it still does.

I should note that the governing board at IPC was made up of women and men, so the idea of women in leadership roles within the church was not the problem. Women were expected to exercise leadership in the church. They made lots of decisions, some spiritual and some practical. They voted on budgets, they set calendars, they created policies and guidelines—in other words, they were elders— but what they were not allowed to do, apparently, was to preach sermons and celebrate the sacraments. These functions were reserved for men.

The United Presbyterian Church in the United States of America, one of the predecessor bodies to the PCUSA, ordained its first woman in 1956, and I have always been glad to be part of a denomination that welcomes the gifts of women. The denomination of my childhood struggled for a few more decades before ordaining its first woman as pastor. To find myself back in a situation where women were kept from a key role in the life of the church was difficult, more so than I had imagined it would be. Many of the members of IPC came from patriarchal cultures and found plenty of support for their cultural attitudes in Switzerland, which denied women the right to vote until 1971. Even so, I had hoped for more.

IN SPITE OF ALL THIS, and not to discount its seriousness, I found these conversations engaging. We were at least talking about theology. It was in Zürich that I began to fall in love with the church again. I fell in love again with the idea of church, with the importance of having core beliefs, with structure and accountability, and with a safety net when things go wrong, as they inevitably do.

I still had a great deal of work to do, but I was beginning to see once again who I was and what was important to me.

Bears and Hyenas and Other Worries

The geographical pilgrimage is the symbolic acting out of an inner journey. The inner journey is the interpolation of the meanings and signs of the outer pilgrimage. One can have one without the other. It is best to have both.

Thomas Merton, *Mystics and Zen Masters*

Aging calls us outdoors, after the adult indoors of work and love-life and keeping stylish, into the lowly simplicities that we thought we had outgrown as children. We come again to love the plain world, its stone and wood, its air and water.

John Updike, *Self-Consciousness: Memoirs*

A YEAR AFTER MY RETIREMENT, I walked the Camino de Santiago in northern Spain. I started my walk in the French village of Saint Jean Pied de Port, at the base of the Pyrenees, and ended five hundred miles and twenty-nine days later in Santiago de Compostela, a cathedral town in northwest Spain. I averaged more than seventeen miles per day, and I took exactly one day off from walking, because I had food poisoning and for hours could barely get out of bed.

Before I set out for Spain, I decided not to write about my pilgrimage. I figured that too much had already been written about the Camino, and there was nothing new I could add. So I left my notebook at home and tried to see and hear as much as humanly possible, without feeling the need to record any of it, a first for me, and easier than I would have expected. I brought along my phone to which I had downloaded a few podcasts, but after listening to just one, a sermon on my first Sunday morning, I deleted the rest. I realized that I was missing too much by concentrating on the voice in my earphones. I wanted to hear instead the crunch of stones under my feet. I wanted to notice the landscape and wildlife. I wanted to smell the soil, some of which had been newly plowed in preparation for planting.

Curiously, I also wanted to sing, something I am not known for doing. I discovered that I knew the first verse to a lot of hymns, and so that's what I sang—the first verse to dozens of hymns, one after another, for what seemed like hours at a time.

The hymn I sang more than any other, the hymn with which I started nearly every day, was "For All the Saints." I knew this hymn so well—every verse of it, in fact—because I had sung it so often, typically as the closing hymn at funeral services. I didn't know what else to do in those situations, standing alongside grieving families, so I would sing the words as loudly as I could:

From earth's wide bounds, from ocean's farthest coast,
Through gates of pearl streams in the countless host,
— Singing to Father, Son, and Holy Ghost.

In the early days of my Camino, when there was no one around,
I sang—not because I didn't know what else to do, but because I
could. Because, after all these years, I thought I knew at last who I was
and what I believed.

Thou art our rock, our fortress, and our might;
Thou, Lord, our captain in the well-fought fight;
Thou, in the darkness drear, our one true light.

After singing the first verse of a hymn, I sometimes found myself
laughing, because I realized that the sight would have been comi-
cal—an old man, carrying a large backpack, singing his fool head
off in the middle of nowhere. But then, after laughing, I sometimes
found myself crying. I thought, "Here I am, on a path in Spain, with
not a single human being for miles around, and I am happy, healthy,
and alive. I am so grateful."

PILGRIMS ARE ENCOURAGED TO SET THEIR INTENTION—their
reason for walking—before starting out. Early on, in the late Middle
Ages, pilgrims would often walk as a form of penance. These days,
I discovered, most pilgrims walk to sort out their lives, to figure out
who they are and where they are going. Some of the lives I heard
about needed a lot of sorting out. A month of solitude and walking
will go a long way toward providing clarity about jobs and relationships, addictions and traumas. A young man from Ireland was walking
with his father, after losing his job and his marriage to alcohol. He
mentioned all of this to me so casually that I was startled, and in my
line of work I was accustomed to hearing confession. But something
about the Camino and this young man's intention to heal from his

trauma allowed him to speak freely and without shame. I enjoyed getting to know him.

Still other pilgrims I met were walking because the Camino was something they had heard about and had always wanted to try. That was partly the case with me too. Few of the pilgrims I met were religious in a conventional way. In fact, they were often quick to point out that they most certainly were not, even before I asked the question.

And yet, the Camino is undeniably a spiritual experience. Tens of thousands, maybe hundreds of thousands, of pilgrims have walked over the centuries, dating back to the ninth century, and every night pilgrim masses in Catholic churches along the way are reminders that the Camino is inseparable from this history.

I decided before leaving that my intention for the pilgrimage would be gratitude. I was going to walk because I was grateful for my life, for my family, for my work as a pastor, and for much more. It was not a hard choice. I had a great deal to be grateful for.

My early days of being utterly alone on the Camino gave way, gradually, to meeting more and more pilgrims, either on the path or in the evening at pilgrim hostels. While resting or doing laundry or eating dinner, we would talk, and one of the first questions, inevitably, would be, "Why are you doing this?" When I told people that I was walking out of a sense of gratitude for my life, I sensed that no one knew quite what to say in response. Not even an "I'm happy for you." So at that point they would tell their own stories, and I listened. I found myself becoming a chaplain to many of those I met, encouraging to them to say more, which was a natural and enjoyable role for me to play. I would ask the people I met about their pilgrimage, and they were happy to tell me, often at great length. I heard wonderful stories. And some sad ones too.

ONE MAN NAMED SEBASTIAN was a Jesuit priest. He was Chilean by birth, but he was living and working in Siberia. He was the founder of a small seminary and responsible for a handful of priests. He also seemed to be the president, academic dean, the entire faculty, and basketball coach. When I first met Sebastian, and he introduced himself as a Jesuit, I said, "Oh, good homilies." To which he replied, with a smile, "Not always." And I thought, "Here's a brother!" I'm not sure he knew what a Presbyterian pastor was, but he seemed to catch on that I was a religious worker of some kind. We walked together for two days, the longest period of time I walked with anyone.

Sebastian's story has stayed with me because of the way he was living out his call to ministry. After receiving a PhD in biblical studies, his superior ordered him to move to Russia. He was not a Russian speaker at the time, though he knew Spanish, French, and English. And as I've discovered in my work abroad, for people who speak more than one language, each additional language seems to be easier to learn than the one before. Still, I found myself asking him, "Did you resist this assignment? Wasn't it a matter of negotiation with your superior?" He seemed puzzled by my questions and told me that he had taken a vow of obedience, along with vows of celibacy and poverty, so of course there was no negotiation about moving to Siberia for the rest of his life.

I wondered what my life would have been like in another religious tradition, if I would have ended up in places like Wheaton, Ann Arbor, or Fort Lauderdale. I decided that the answer, most likely, was no.

One evening in a village church, at the pilgrim mass, I sat next to Sebastian and heard him making disapproving noises during the homily. I understood little of what the village priest was saying, but Sebastian was clearly irritated. My sense was that the priest hadn't put much effort into it, was phoning it in, and this irritated Sebastian, who, as I knew from our conversations, set high standards for himself and his students. We went forward together for the wafer and returned to our seats. The next night, Sebastian stopped in a small town and found a community of Jesuits where he planned to spend the night. I kept going and never met up with him again, something that happened often along the Camino.

MEETING SEBASTIAN AND OTHERS LIKE HIM was the high point of my pilgrimage. The low point occurred the first night.

I stayed overnight in Saint Jean Pied de Port after my arrival in Europe. My plan was to stop at the post office in the morning before setting off on my first day of walking. I wanted to mail some clothes and other travel items ahead to Santiago, rather than carry these items with me. My backpack, I figured, was already heavy enough. But the post office didn't open until 9:00, and by the time I sealed up the box and paid for the postage, I was already well behind in my day. I was still a little jet-lagged too, having arrived in Paris the day before and taken a train to Saint Jean. I should probably have spent the day resting and looking around the quaint medieval town, but there was no holding me back after months of planning and training. And so, foolishly, I set out.

The day turned out to be unseasonably warm for the end of February. At the warmest point of the day, the temperature reached into the mid-80s, and though I knew the first day involved a moderate-to-difficult climb, getting to the top of the Pyrenees nearly did me in. The snow was melting at higher elevations, and when I ran out of water, I had to drink out of a mountain stream, something I most definitely would not have done under other circumstances. By late afternoon I figured I was at least three to four kilometers from the monastery at Roncesvalles where I had planned to stay my first night. The sun was going down, and I began to worry about getting lost in the forest and losing my way in the dark. I tried to make a calm and rational decision, which was to stop and spend the night on the ground next to the path. But I was worried. I had no idea how many wild animals lived here and how safe I would be without a tent or shelter of any kind.

I spread my rain poncho on the ground, the only time I was to need it for the entire walk. I rolled out my sleeping bag on top of that, thankful to have a bag that would keep me warm even if the temperature dropped below freezing, as it eventually did. I even brushed my teeth. I never camp, so I didn't know what else I was supposed to do. I had no food. I had a good grip on one of my hiking poles, though, just in case I had to use it to fight off a bear or hyena or whatever lived in these woods. And then I waited to fall asleep.

No one knew where I was. My phone was useless without Wi-Fi. I had no way of contacting anyone, and my screams would not have been heard. I was scared. I worried that my half-eaten body would be found in a few days and people would say, "That sure was a stupid thing to do." African American friends have told me that they are often afraid, especially of police during traffic stops. As a white man, I can't remember the last time I was afraid. I was probably six or seven years old and afraid of dogs. But there has been nothing like that until this night.

If any bears or hyenas sniffed around that night, I don't remember. I woke a few times, but always went back to sleep. I woke for good around 6:00. I walked the last few kilometers and stopped for breakfast in Roncesvalles. I was barely twenty-four hours into my pilgrimage, and I had already faced my worst fear which, like many fears, turned out to be nothing much at all.

A PILGRIMAGE, IT IS SAID, consists of both an inward and an outward journey. Getting to Santiago on foot, avoiding serious injuries and blisters, and having my picture taken in front of the famous cathedral was the outward journey. The inward journey was, as always, a bit more complicated.

Not all pilgrims start out in France. Many of them start much closer to Santiago. If you walk a hundred kilometers (about 60 miles), you get the same certificate at the end as if you had started where I did, on the wrong side of the Pyrenees. As more and more people joined the pilgrimage, I remember feeling a twinge of resentment. Some of them had jobs to return to, of course, and couldn't afford to be away from home for a month or more. Others found it more convenient to start at cities like Pamplona, especially those who had flown into Madrid, not Paris. I knew all of the reasons people gave for where they started their walk, but as I listened I found myself feeling superior to them, as though I was the real pilgrim and they were merely pretenders.

I was even irritated when I would meet up with pilgrims during the day who had no backpack, because they had paid a few euros to have it sent ahead by taxi to the next town. It would be there waiting for them at the end of the day, and that, I must say, seemed like cheating to me, taking the easy way. Other pilgrims, I discovered, never stayed in pilgrim hostels—or *albergues*—but instead found small hotels along the way where they had bathrooms to themselves and comfortable beds. I confess that after the midway point, I was looking to stay at hotels too, whenever I could find them, in order to avoid the snoring at night in the dormitory-style sleeping areas. But I felt smug anyway.

I felt ashamed of myself for having these thoughts at the same time I was having them. I knew at some level that none of it mattered. I walked as far as I did for my own reasons. No one was keeping score. There is no right or wrong way to walk a pilgrimage. There is no right or wrong way to spend the night. A pilgrimage is utterly personal, and so each one is different. I was responsible only for my own. But the Camino had revealed to me that I can be petty and self-righteous, that I make judgments about other people all the time, even when I know better. I had approached the Camino the same way I had approached my life as a pastor: I wanted to succeed at it, as though ministry can be rewarded with a gold medal.

I would say that walking all day, every day, for a month, reveals a person, the good and the bad. I like to think that no one can see my flaws, but the truth is, my fellow pilgrims probably had to put up with a great deal when they were with me. I am grateful that they walked with me anyway. I had to walk with myself, and that was enough.

AFTER THE NIGHT ON THE MOUNTAIN with the wild animals, the most challenging part of the Camino for me was spending so much time alone.

For most of my life, I have not been alone. I have been with my wife, or my children, or my friends, or members of my church. I can see now that I tried hard over the years not to be alone. I tend to be quiet and reserved in social settings, but personality tests reveal that I am an extrovert. Given the choice, I prefer being with other people as opposed to being alone. But on the Camino I was frequently alone for most of each day. I even ate in restaurants alone, something I had never done in the United States. I had not had so much alone time since I lived in a single room on the third floor of Alexander Hall during my first two years at Princeton Seminary. I spent a lot of time alone there too, even though I was surrounded by other students.

Before leaving for Spain, I talked with a few people who had already walked the Camino, and they warned me about the Meseta, the vast plain in central Spain. One of them even encouraged me to take a bus and avoid the entire thing, a hundred miles or so of flat, monotonous land. Beginning just after Burgos, and ending in Astorga, the Spanish Meseta can be an unforgiving experience. I took several photos with my phone of the gravel path in front of me that seemed to stretch in a straight line all the way to the horizon.

Looking back, I'm glad I didn't take a bus. I walked alone, and I found that I enjoyed being alone, which was for me a good and surprising discovery, maybe the most surprising discovery of the entire experience. I've heard old bromides like "if you make friends with yourself, you'll never be lonely," and I suppose there is some truth to all of them, but my aloneness on the Camino served a different function.

I can now see that on the Camino I was in recovery from forty years as a pastor. I was learning to be myself again after all those years of playing a role. On the Camino I felt free to be myself and to discover once again who I am. I was friendly, but I didn't need friends. I was interested in the pilgrims I met, but I didn't depend on them to make my Camino a good experience. I learned to depend on myself for that. I learned to think my own thoughts, at my own pace, and in no particular order. I thought about some important relationships in my life and how they could be different when I returned. I thought about a book project and organized it in my mind. I reviewed much of my ministry, remembering the good moments and acknowledging the bad ones.

Henry David Thoreau famously lived alone for two years, two months, and two days in a small house next to Walden Pond in Concord, Massachusetts. He was never truly alone, though. He had many visitors and even writes about always having three chairs available for them. He remarks at one point in his book that he always had more company at Walden Pond than he did in the city. He also made several trips each week into Concord where he bought supplies and spoke with townspeople and traded gossip. But even with all of the human interaction, he was alone much of the time and wrote about the feeling of solitude, which he seems to have enjoyed. He found that a deep communion with nature was often preferable to the company of friends. The "only medicine" he needed, he wrote, was "a draught of morning air."

I loved reading *Walden* when I was a high school student, and now I remember why. Solitude, along with a contemplative life and a few possessions, makes for a better, richer life. For a month I carried everything I needed on my back. And now I know that, if I had to, I could get by with much less. My possessions seldom add much richness to my life. I am grateful for what I have, of course, but I live with the knowledge that I don't need those things to make me happy.

I also know that I enjoy having family and friends around; I love to listen to them talk and laugh. But here's the thing: I don't need them to fill an empty place.

My life is full at last, and I am grateful for that.

19

Chasing after Wind

I have the persistent sensation, in my life and art, that I am just beginning. But, no, I am near the end.

John Updike, *Self-Consciousness: Memoirs*

But the sad and well-known fact of the matter is that most of us will stay in our caskets and be dead a long time, and that our urns and graves will never make a sound.

Thomas Lynch, *The Undertaking:*
Life Studies from the Dismal Trade

IN MY FIRST MONTHS OF RETIREMENT, I was surprised to find myself plunged into a life review that I didn't expect and didn't want, but somehow couldn't avoid. Suddenly, for the first time in decades, I had time to think, and I remember thinking about everything, not just my work, but my relationships, my family, and my faith. I have since read that many people who are my age engage in a life review like this, sometimes requiring the help of a therapist.

Erik Erikson, the twentieth-century psychologist, identified eight stages or crises (toward the end of his life he added a ninth stage) that we must resolve in order to achieve emotional or mental health. He identifies the eighth stage as "ego integrity versus despair." The "crisis" (his term) that needs to be resolved requires a look back, a remembering, of one's life in order to achieve contentedness and serenity and perhaps even wisdom.

One afternoon in March, on a gray Michigan day, not long after arriving back in the United States, I spent a few hours going through boxes I had dragged with me around the country, move after move, five states in all. I even paid to store them in a "climate-controlled, manager-on-site" facility while I lived and worked in Europe. I always assumed that one day, probably in retirement, I would finally go through everything, though that day always seemed like a long way off. Musty-smelling and battered, though still remarkably intact, the boxes were covered with a familiar handwriting, a younger, more confident version of mine today. With a black marker I had carefully identified what was in each box.

To get the work started, my wife volunteered to go through the boxes with me. This seemed like a wise plan. She had no sentimental feelings, for example, about the college literary magazine I had helped to edit during my senior year and all of the copies I carefully saved in order of their publication. My wife seemed delighted, in fact, at the prospect of "getting rid of some things," as she put it. She promised that I could save one or two reminders from my past that would fit on the bookshelves above the desk in my home office.

At first, the opening and sorting and tossing seemed manageable enough, but I soon realized that this was not going to be a half-day project. As it turned out, each item had to be examined. Each photo required close examination. Each letter had to be read and reread. "Who in the world is that person in the photo?" "Why did I save this?" On and on, it went.

Then, suddenly, my wife held up a photo and said, "Isn't this one with you and your old girlfriend?" She thought she was being funny, but the question hurt. I took the photo and studied it. I didn't remember when it was taken, but the photo was of me and a person I met and dated when I was in college. The relationship, which had been moving toward marriage, ended abruptly, because I, in my immaturity and fear, had broken it off. And suddenly there I was, decades later, in my basement, up to my knees in open boxes, overwhelmed with guilt and remorse.

"I should apologize to her," I said. And my wife agreed, "You should."

I did apologize to her, in the weeks that followed, after I thought carefully about what I should say and how I should say it. Through the dubious miracle of social media, she was easier to find than I expected and more gracious about hearing from me than I deserved. There may be still other confessions and apologies as my life review continues.

MOSTLY, THOUGH, MY LIFE REVIEW has been about my life as a pastor, and I kept coming to the conclusion that I, like my Grandma Brouwer, spent a lot of my life chasing after wind, that in the end my work didn't add up to much.

When I mentioned this to friends and seminary classmates, when I began to share first drafts of this book with them, I found that the first impulse for many of them was to talk me out of it, to remind me of all the "good" that I accomplished throughout my career. One person even shared with me what he called his "exit interview," a snappy PowerPoint presentation that showcased his life and career and the (mostly) happy outcomes he enjoyed along the way. I did my best to listen to all of this. I had asked for feedback, after all, and I wanted to believe what I was being told. But as I listened I realized that these friends were also trying to convince themselves that their own careers had been worthwhile, that they, too, had accomplished much that was "good." If they had agreed with me, even a little, then that agreement would have cast doubt on the worthiness of their own lives as pastors.

In one of these conversations, a friend, one who has mounted his own brutally honest life review, reminded me of seminary classmates who did not serve large churches, who devoted themselves instead to lives of service, often in small towns, often without financial reward. I found this response to be more compelling, and his reminiscing led to reminiscing of my own.

I remember one classmate, in particular, who never seemed to me to have much of a future as a pastor. I could be judgmental during my seminary years, as I can be now, and I judged this classmate to have little potential for success, as I defined it then. Even with a decent haircut and better suit and speech coach, he was never going to fit my image of a pastor who was going places, by which I meant of course Fifth Avenue Presbyterian Church in New York City. And then, not long ago, this classmate reconnected with me through social media, and I discovered that he has lived his life as a pastor in some remarkable ways—in ways I now envy, in fact. His life as a pastor has revealed courage and integrity and depth. If there is room for one more of those plaques outside the dining hall at Princeton Seminary, plaques that honor graduates who gave their lives in heroic service, this classmate deserves to be there. I didn't see it then, but I see it now.

FINDING A CHURCH IN RETIREMENT turned out to be much harder than I expected, which is remarkable since there are around 170 churches in the small town where I now live, an astonishing number. I didn't visit all of them, but I found my way to a few of them, and in the end decided to spend my Sunday mornings with Presbyterians, the people with whom I've spent the most time over the years. In a community with so many descendants of the Dutch migration, there are many Reformed and Christian Reformed churches, leaving little room for the Scottish branch of the Reformation in which I served for forty years. But there is one such church, and I landed there.

Early on I sat in the back and hurried out immediately after the benediction. I avoided coffee hour and congregational meetings, mostly because I could. After a few months, though, I came to know the pastor and told her that I wanted to support and encourage her. I have preached a few times for her too, often on holiday weekends, so that she could get away. I've been grateful for those opportunities, and I've been surprised by how much I enjoyed them. When I asked how I could show my support, her response was simple and straight-forward: "Show up." I think back to the churches I've served over the years and find myself grateful for all of the people who supported me by showing up week after week, usually taking the same seat in the same row. Whenever the church doors opened, they were there. They read the prayers in the order of worship, they opened their hymn-books when I announced a hymn, and they passed the offering plate when it was handed to them. I should have acknowledged what a gift their presence was.

I still sit in the back when I'm not preaching, and I have come to know a few of the people who sit near me. We talk and ask about each other's health before worship begins. The wife of one of the men who sits near me died. I remember hearing the announcement in worship one Sunday and decided to "show up" for the memorial service, even though I didn't know either of them very well. A lot of church life is about showing up.

I even joined the men's book discussion group and started to attend their monthly meetings. The members of the group, like the members of the church, are older. I am the youngest member of the group, and though I'm not the youngest member of the church, I am on the younger side. This, of course, is not a good sign. Before the COVID-19 pandemic, I wondered if this church would be around in twenty years, and now I wonder if the church will be around in five. The Presbyterian church that I attend, as is happening in many places, is getting older and smaller, and it will most likely disappear. The older members will hang on until they can no longer afford to pay a pastor, and then the decision will be made to close the doors and sell the property. Years ago, I would have been sad to hear a story like that, and now I think it's okay. That congregation has had a good run and has done a great deal that was "good." Now it may be time for it to close its doors and go away. With 169 others to choose from, no one should feel too bad.

The church I attend most Sundays, to its credit, has taken a progressive stance toward most issues. Clearly stated on the church website is its openness to gay and lesbian people: "Whatever your background, exposure to Christianity, or sexual orientation, you are welcome here!" Even an exclamation point! No church I served over the years was ready to offer a welcome like that, which I regret, but the open arms of the church in Holland have not led to growth and full pews and a Sunday school teeming with children and young families, all the indicators of success that I adopted during my forty years of ministry. But there is courage and integrity in standing for something, and I admire that.

I will continue to show up on Sunday, and I will continue to imagine what ministry might look like when it is freed from most of the expectations I once had.

A YEAR AND A HALF AFTER MOVING BACK to the United States from Switzerland, and four months after returning from the Camino de Santiago in northern Spain, I received an email from a church in Lucerne, Switzerland. Their pastor had just resigned and moved to Germany, and a couple of members who knew me had given my name to the elders. Would I be interested, they wondered, in serving as interim pastor, from late August to Christmas, long enough for them to complete their search for a new pastor?

I surprised myself by saying yes, and with only one suitcase I flew to the Zürich airport where the chairperson of the church board met me and drove me to Lucerne. I traveled alone, and the plan was for my wife to visit me briefly at some point during the fall. The elders seemed to like this plan because it meant that they had to pay for only one airfare. The salary they offered was low compared to churches I had served previously, but the apartment provided by the church may have been one of the best in the city. I enjoyed a spectacular view of Mount Pilatus from my living room window (on days when the mountain wasn't enveloped in clouds).

I was the only staff member at the church in Lucerne, and my responsibilities, beyond Sunday morning worship, included typing and copying the weekly worship bulletin, typing and mailing the weekly e-newsletter, teaching two weekly Bible studies, and just about everything else. I joked to one person that I may have been responsible for vacuuming the sanctuary, and if that was the case, I never got around to it. I was busy, but not too busy. I was challenged, but hardly overwhelmed. For the first time that I could remember, I was aware that I was comfortable in my own skin. I knew who I was at last and what I could (and couldn't) do for them. Thankfully, I wasn't concerned about adding anything to my résumé.

My congregation in Lucerne, as it had been in Zürich, was multiracial and multiethnic. I was one of the few Americans and native English speakers in the congregation. The rest of the members were from all over the world. There were no lake baptisms, but one older woman from China, with a doctorate in traditional Chinese medicine, came to faith during my time at the church. Sadly, I had to return to the United States before she was baptized, or I would have gladly waded out into Lake Lucerne and helped raise her to new life.

Our average attendance on Sundays was 120 people. Members seemed pleased that we had to open the room divider, which separated the worship space from the coffee hour space, in order to set up more folding chairs. (Old standards die hard.) Rather than stand in the pulpit, I stood at floor level and preached my sermons from a music stand. I had not let go of my need for a manuscript, but after forty years of public speaking I was finally able to stand close to my audience and make eye contact with every single person, which I thought of as a remarkable achievement, like learning at long last to hit a baseball out of the infield.

The church had been through "a difficult season of ministry" by the time I arrived (that artful expression again), they had parted ways with their previous pastor in a way that didn't feel right to anyone, and they were eager for someone to lead them, to love them, to visit them when they were sick—in other words, they were eager for someone to be their pastor.

While I was there, one family observed the first anniversary of the death of their three-, almost four-year-old son named Skylar. He had been struck and killed by a car, and the congregation—in many ways an extended family—was devastated. As is often the case, no one knew what to say, and everyone feared saying the wrong thing, with the result that no one said anything at all. I took a bus to visit the family one evening. I spent time in their apartment getting to know each of them, and I listened as they told their story of unimaginable grief one more time. Together, we made a plan to remember their son, both at a mountaintop observance on Saturday evening and then again in worship on Sunday morning. I don't know if what we did was exactly right, but it was what they wanted and what the church members needed. We cried, we laughed (a little), and we watched a video during worship that Skylar's father had put together for the occasion. Remarkably, we were able to smile through our tears, which turned out to be yet another holy moment in my life, and I had no trouble explaining why it was holy.

In that moment, as a matter of fact, I felt as though I had come full circle in my work. When I was in Iowa City, between my second and third years of seminary training, I served a small church, which also acted like an extended family, meaning that they fought sometimes, made up after a while, and got along most of the time. I caught a glimpse all those years ago of what it meant to be a pastor, and, based on what I saw, I felt called to be that person. I returned to seminary with vocational clarity. I knew—or thought I knew—what I had been called to do and to be with my life.

Then, soon after my ordination, I lost my way. I got caught up in my career and nearly always followed my ambition more than my call. I blame the seminary, of course, for dangling in front of me and my classmates a model of ministry that turned out to be dated and not what the times demanded. I blame the Presbyterian Church, too, for acting more like Xerox and IBM, and not enough like a mom and pop store, which is probably what the church needs to be. And I blame myself for getting caught up in a world that never felt authentic to me, for allowing my careerism to get in the way of my happiness, and for forgetting the holy bits, which I had been ordained to touch and to tell others about.

So, over the years, yes, I spent a lot of time chasing after wind. A regrettably long time. I also regret not having had the courage at important times to speak the truth, to use my position and my authority to speak for those who couldn't speak for themselves. In the end, though, the grace that found me in Iowa City all those years ago never left me. I still feel loved, in spite of it all, and that love still feels unearned and undeserved.

Somebody loving you that much is grace. The people I came to know in my work (most of them) were grace. The staff members who worked side by side with me were grace. The mission trips, the hospital visits, the leadership retreats, the church board meetings, and all those Friday mornings spent writing sermons—they were all grace. My life has been full to overflowing with grace.

Sometimes, when I remember where I've been and what I was allowed to do, I begin to cry.

Acknowledgments

I sat next to my father in worship every Sunday for nearly eighteen years, morning and evening services. (My family seldom, if ever, missed a Sunday, no matter what was going on in our lives or in the world.) I listened to my father sing and pray. I watched as he placed his envelope in the offering plate each week. I watched him receive communion and serve the church as an elder. Because of both my parents, Jack and Ruth Brouwer, I can't remember a time when I did not believe, when faith was not at the center of my life. My parents made sure that, from the day I was born, I was steeped and soaked and marinated in the Christian faith.

My kindergarten Sunday school teacher at the Plymouth Heights Christian Reformed Church, where I grew up, was Mrs. Peterson. She made the Bible stories come alive for me in a way no one else ever has, including some highly regarded seminary professors with whom I studied. She had a first name—someone once told me it was Alice—but to me she will always be Mrs. Peterson.

Mrs. DeJong, my fifth-grade teacher at Sylvan Christian School, more than likely had a first name as well, but whatever it was she will also always be Mrs. DeJong to me. I remember her because, of all my elementary school teachers (and some of those who came after), I knew that she understood me. She also somehow made a student out of me and let me know that I could write a good story.

Richard Mouw, PhD, was for me and many others a memorable and engaging teacher, and I am grateful for his classes at Calvin College, where he taught before leaving for Fuller Theological Seminary. It was in Princeton, New Jersey, where he and his wife Phyllis had gone for a sabbatical year, that I found the courage to call him Rich for the first time. I am grateful for all the ways he tried to point me in the right direction.

William H. Nibbelink, PhD—or Bill, as he was known at the Trinity Christian Reformed Church in Iowa City, Iowa, where he was an elder—became my advisor and friend at a time when I needed all the advising and friendship I could get. I will always be grateful.

The Rev. Fred R. Anderson was the first person with whom I interviewed on the Princeton Seminary campus when I was looking for my first call after seminary as an assistant pastor. I had never met anyone quite like Fred, and I have never met anyone quite like him in the years since. Fred was responsible for the best first five years in ministry a new pastor ever had.

Meeting and getting to know Father Elias Chacour turned out to be one of the most important experiences of my life. Father Chacour, who later became Archbishop of Galilee in the Melkite Greek Catholic Church, founded a school for Jews, Arabs, Christians, and Druze in the tiny village of Ibillin in northern Israel. In him I was able to imagine the strength and courage that Jesus once had in standing up to earthly powers with nothing more than (and nothing less than) the conviction that he was doing God's work.

AT AN EARLY STAGE IN THE WRITING of this book, several people, including friends, classmates, and family members, cheerfully agreed to read at least two chapters (and in several cases the entire manuscript) and offer feedback. I wish I could give more detail about how I know each of them and how important they are to me. In alphabetical order: the Rev. Thomas W. Blair, the Rev.

Acknowledgments

Sarah D. Brouwer, Elizabeth Brouwer, PhD, Jolene Carpenter, the Rev. Thomas B. Dozeman, PhD, the Rev. Charlotte Ellison, the Rev. Linda Hart Green, the Rev. John C. Hage, Marvin L. Hage, MD, the Rev. Lawrence A. Jones, the Rev. Kate VanNoord Kooyman, the Rev. Patricia Locke, the Rev. Stephens G. Lytch, Karen Randles, Debra Rienstra, PhD, Mark Schumacher, Mary R. Talen, PhD, and John Whittier-Ferguson, PhD.

I ALSO INTERVIEWED SEVERAL PEOPLE in the course of my writing, mostly to compare and contrast my memories of certain events. I promised not to quote them, but I am grateful for their candid insights into our common experiences: The Rev. M. Craig Barnes, PhD (current president of Princeton Theological Seminary), the Rev. John M. Mulder, PhD (former faculty member at Princeton Theological Seminary and former president of Louisville Presbyterian Theological Seminary), and Jon Pott (former vice president and editor-in-chief at Wm. B. Eerdmans Publishing Company).

MY ASSOCIATION WITH the Wm. B. Eerdmans Publishing Company dates to the early 1970s when I landed a summer job in what was then the sales promotion department. My first book with Eerdmans, *Remembering the Faith*, was published in 1999. It's hard to overstate how proud I am that *Chasing after Wind* is my fifth book with such a fine company. The women and men I have worked with over the years have always been thoughtful, kind, and generous, and I will always be grateful.

IN CHILDHOOD MY WIFE NEVER IMAGINED herself marrying a pastor, just as I never imagined myself becoming one, but together we became a pretty good team, reluctantly at first and then later unreservedly. Along the way, Susan taught Sunday school, sang in the church choir, directed a children's choir, led women's retreats, served as an elder, listened to church members who needed someone to unburden themselves with, lip-synced Diana Ross's "Stop! In the Name of Love" at a talent show (and mission fundraiser), and once even directed an elaborate children's Christmas pageant that featured live animals. She did all of this while raising two daughters and practicing law full-time for more than twenty-five years. Even more remarkably, she listened patiently to me whenever I needed someone who would listen, which was quite often. (She came out of her retirement as a pastor's wife to read and approve the final draft of this book.)